The
Canary
Islander

Barrie Mahoney worked as a teacher and head teacher in the south west of England, and then became a school inspector in England and Wales. A new life and career as a newspaper reporter in Spain's Costa Blanca led to him launching and editing an English language newspaper in the Canary Islands. Barrie's books include novels in 'The Prior's Hill Chronicles' series, as well as books for expats in the 'Letters from the Atlantic' series, which give an amusing and reflective view of life abroad.

Barrie writes regular columns for newspapers and magazines in Spain, Portugal, Ireland, Australia, South Africa, Canada, UK and the USA. He also designs websites to promote the Canary Islands and living and working abroad, and is often asked to contribute to radio programmes about expat life.

Visit the author's websites:

http://barriemahoney.com
http://thecanaryislander.com

Other books by Barrie Mahoney

Journeys & Jigsaws (The Canary Islander Publishing) 2013
ISBN: 978-0957544475 (Paperback and eBook)

Threads and Threats (The Canary Islander Publishing) 2013
ISBN: 978-0992767105 (Paperback and eBook)

Letters from the Atlantic (The Canary Islander Publishing) 2013
ISBN: 978-0992767136 (Paperback and eBook)

Living the Dream (The Canary Islander Publishing) 2015
ISBN: 978-0992767198 (Paperback and eBook)

Expat Survival (The Canary Islander Publishing) 2015
ISBN: 978-0992767167 (Paperback and eBook)

Message in a Bottle (The Canary Islander Publishing) 2016
ISBN: 978-0995602700 (Paperback and eBook)

Escape to the Sun (The Canary Islander Publishing) 2016
ISBN: 978-0957544444 (Paperback and eBook)

Expat Voice (The Canary Islander Publishing) 2014
ISBN: 978-0992767174 (Paperback and eBook)

Island in the Sun (The Canary Islander Publishing) 2015
ISBN: 978-0992767181 (Paperback and eBook)

Footprints in the Sand (The Canary Islander Publishing) 2016 ISBN: 978-0995602717 (Paperback and eBook)

Living in Spain and the Canary Islands (The Canary Islander Publishing) 2017 ISBN: 978-0995602724 (Paperback and eBook)

Letters from the Canary Islands and Spain

Barrie Mahoney

The Canary Islander Publishing

© Copyright 2018

Barrie Mahoney

The right of Barrie Mahoney to be identified as author of this work has been asserted by him in accordance with the Copyright, Designs and Patents Act 1988.

All Rights Reserved

No reproduction, copy or transmission of this publication may be made without written permission. No paragraph of this publication may be reproduced, copied or transmitted save with the written permission of the author, or in accordance with the provisions of the Copyright Act 1956 (as amended).
Any person who commits any unauthorised act in relation to this publication may be liable to criminal prosecution and civil claims for damages.
A CIP catalogue record for this title is available from the British Library.

ISBN 978-0995602731
www.barriemahoney.com

First Published in 2018

The Canary Islander Publishing

Acknowledgements

I would like to thank all those people that I have met on my journey to where I am now.

To supportive friends who helped me to overcome the many problems and frustrations that I faced and taught me much about learning to adapt to a new culture. Also, to friends in the UK, or scattered around the world, who have kept in touch despite being so far away.

To the people that I met whilst working as a newspaper reporter and editor in Spain and the Canary Islands, and for the privilege of sharing their successes and challenges in life.

Disclaimer

This is a book about real people, real places and real events, but names of people and companies have been changed to avoid any embarrassment.

DEDICATION

This book is dedicated to people all over the world who dream of a new life, new experiences, new cultures, new opportunities to experience, taste and smell the excitement of a place that is of their own choosing and not merely based upon an accident of birth.

Contents	12
Preface	15
A Dose of Culture	20
Alice in Blunderland	21
Crackers and Crappers	24
La Boda	28
For the Love of Paper	31
What's in a Name?	34
The Russia Connection	36
Staying Healthy	39
Overweight 'Bridegrooms of Death'	40
Kill or Cure?	43
All Helmets and Lycra	46
An Appointment for an Appointment	49
Avoid the Doctor, Eat Honey	53
Sunbeds R Us	56
An Elderly Expat Dog	59
Life and Death	62
Don't Shoot the Messenger	63
The Cost of Expats Dying	66
Ashes to Ashes	69
Communicating with Beer and Stones	72
Do You Speak English?	73
Learn a Language with Beer and Insomnia	76
Linguaphobia	78

Stoned	81
Food, Wine and Shopping	84
Chickpeas or Coco Pops for Breakfast?	85
Chocolate, Avocado Eggs and the Canary Islands	88
Just Nuts About Almonds	91
Red, White or Blue?	94
Up the Amazon	96
Dog Gate	100
The 'B' Word	104
Brexit and the Faint-Hearted Expat	105
The Journey of Life	108
Eleven Women and One Astronaut	111
There's No Such Thing as a Free Lunch	114
Brexit Going Bananas	118
A Traitor in Paradise	120
Getting Used to the Unexpected	123
The Virtual Spanish Hotel	124
Bed and Breakfast, but No Roof	127
It's a Crazy, Crazy Expat August	130
No Home in the Sun	134
Poverty in the Canary Islands	135
Living in a Hayloft or a Pod	139
It's Very Easy to be Conned	143
Unemployment Good, Employment Bad	147
The Great Spain Pension Robbery	150
Fuel Poverty	153

Use It or Lose It	156
Timples and Traditions	160
A Little More Than Amnesia	161
Celebrating Canaries Day	164
Let's Thresh a Lentil	168
Calima – Gone With the Wind	171
Documentoscopia	174
Anyone for a Timple?	177
Lizards, Lottery and Lanzarote	180
Getting to Know a Lizard	181
Win a House for Five Euros!	183
The Motor of the Atlantic	186
Lottery and Lanzarote	190

Preface

Preface

As is the custom in the 'Letters from the Atlantic' series, this book includes letters written over a one-year period from the Canary Islands. These letters are inspired by my life in the Canary Islands and Spain and are intended for all those who love these beautiful islands and the country that it is part of.

The winter months have now set in, and much of Europe is currently facing chilly temperatures, rain, heavy cloud and even snow. As I write this on a sunny, warm morning in November, I am reminded of those words uttered by Christopher Columbus when he referred to these island as "The Fortunate Isles"; they certainly are.

Despite living in what I have come to appreciate as one of the best places on Earth to live and work, these islands are not always the paradise that many claim them to be. In my weekly letters, I try to give a balanced and honest view of living on these islands, which is why I sometimes write about poverty and food banks, high unemployment, lack of affordable housing, the migrant crisis, physical and mental abuse, animal cruelty, robbery, murder, and drug and alcohol abuse to name just a few of the human conditions that impact upon this 'paradise'.

These disturbing reports often surprise readers and I occasionally receive indignant emails from island lovers who wish to express their displeasure about my more 'negative letters'. "You should focus on the best things about these lovely islands", I am told. "We don't want to read about island misery; we get enough of that at home", I was told recently by a visiting tourist.

I do not work for the tourist industry, nor the islands' government. My aim, as always, is to try and give an unbiased and informed view of real life on these islands and Spain, and not to reflect the often dishonest, yet idyllic pictures in all those holiday brochures.

Sorry to shatter illusions of near paradise, but life here is just not like that. Whilst most of those 'all inclusive' glass palaces are owned and managed by overseas business interests, it is local people who have to work long, unsocial hours, often with low pay and poor working conditions to ensure that our overseas visitors have an enjoyable and memorable holiday.

For those who live and work in the Canary Islands and Spain, as well as other European countries, the looming spectre of Brexit has, for many, created a troublesome year. The future of Brits living in European Union countries remains uncertain, although all hope that common sense and pragmatism will eventually prevail for the benefit of everyone.

The dream that myself and many others were able to fulfil of living and working in any European country and not to be restrained by location due an accident of birth, looks as if it will be denied to others in the future. Work and residency permits, driven by the need to restrict migration, which most had thought had long gone, have once again raised their ugly heads. The freedoms that we have been able to enjoy in the last forty years or so, look as if they are about to change. Only time will tell whether Brexit was a wise and successful strategy or not.

On a more positive note, this book aims to celebrate what I and many others enjoy about living in these wonderful islands, as well as Spain. It has been a joy this year to find that the islands' government has found ways of significantly reducing the costs for residents to travel across all the islands, as well as to the Spanish Peninsular.

This strategy is helping residents across all the islands to discover the many unique features of each island, as well as the opportunity to travel to Peninsular Spain, which has previously been denied to them, because of high travel costs. In addition, most of the islands are now offering heavily discounted tickets for internal travel, which is helping the unemployed to seek jobs further afield, students to access higher education, as well helping older people to explore and socialise.

On a more personal note, these islands are for me a paradise, and I could not imagine living anywhere else. When I first visited the Canary Islands on a package holiday so many years ago, I knew that one day, somehow, I would live here.

I have been fortunate, the UK being a member of the European Union has certainly helped, as did my career change from teacher to reporter. Life is short, and I hope that in some small way, this book, as well as other books in the 'Letters from the Atlantic' series will help to inspire and motivate others to 'seek and live their dream'.

A Dose of Culture

Alice in Blunderland

Well, it is panto season again, so I have to use a panto title that broadly fits into the spirit of the season, don't I? If you feel like shouting "Oh yes he did", or "Oh no he didn't", please feel free. I really won't be offended.

Do you ever feel that you have stepped into an alternative universe, or into an Alice in Wonderland situation? I certainly do, and I have been aware of it more in 2017 than any other year that I can remember. Post Truth, Fake News, Trump, 'Little Rocket Man' and Brexit have all added to a period of uncertainty and confusion that makes many of us ask if reality, as we know it, is finally spinning out of control?

Currently, it seems that change, accompanied by chaos and confusion, is the order of the day and we had better get used to it. It is within this theme that I am going to suggest an idea that will add a little more chaos and confusion. How about visiting a Spanish town where they talk backwards for your holiday this year?

A flight to the lovely Canary island of Tenerife and a trip to the town of La Laguna could be just the place to visit in our new 'Alice in Wonderland' world. Here visitors will witness, and maybe experience, first-hand the Verres language, which is the only place in the world where they speak back to front.

I guess it could be compared to rhyming slang used in English, or a version of Pig Latin. Verres is not to be treated as a joke or taken too lightly, since enthusiasts in La Laguna are currently asking UNESCO to consider making it an 'Intangible Cultural Heritage'.

Verres started life in a barber's shop in La Laguna in the 1930s. The barber, Francisco Fariña, started using the language mainly to entertain and joke with customers whilst he cut their hair. In the 1930s, La Laguna was a sleepy town with very little going on, and people went to the barber's shop to read the paper, gossip and put the world to rights.

Being quite a wag, Francisco invented a new way of taking scrambled letters and syllables of words to confuse customers, particularly from the rural areas, whom he liked to tease. Francisco's language became so popular in his day that even students from the University of La Laguna began to 'study' the language with him in his barber shop 'academy'.

Verres is currently spoken by around 60 residents of the town and is regarded as an amusing way of talking to friends. It is currently becoming more popular with its cultural heritage being taught and discussed in schools. Although dismissed as little more than a linguistic game by some, others point out that it has its own rules, whilst others use the language in their singing.

Currently, the European Union has 24 official languages and claims to be in favour of linguistic diversity across all of its member states. Maybe one day, Verres will also be included as one of its working languages. Well, I did say that we are stepping into an alternative universe, so why not?

History teaches us that chaos and confusion happen from time to time in all civilisations. Although I am not too keen on the chaos part of stepping into an alternative universe, I always like a new challenge. I know that many embrace change and long for a correction to an imperfect world order as they see it.

As individuals, I guess that there is little that we can do about it, other than to embrace change and see the positive side of what it has to offer and to keep an open mind. I wonder what Alice would have to say about it all? Happy New Year, or I should say, Yppah Wen Raey!

Crackers and Crappers at Christmas

It is often difficult for people who move to Spain to leave behind many of the traditions that they are used to in their home countries, and instead to adopt some new traditions in their host country. For many, the traditions of the Christmas festive period (or Navidades as it is called in Spain) are a major adjustment. It is important to remember that Spain is a Catholic country, and for many Spanish people, the Christmas period is still an important religious holiday that is celebrated regardless of faith.

The first sign of Christmas is usually the Christmas Belén that appear in churches, shopping centres and large department stores. This is the traditional nativity scene that tells the Christmas story through often beautiful, intricate model displays; the best ones will keep children entertained for some time!

For more adult entertainment, watch out for the 'crappers', which is a popular addition to the nativity scene. This is usually a figure perched behind Mary and Joseph seated in a defecating position. Usually, these figures represent politicians and sporting heroes, popular or otherwise. Many British readers will be proud to recall that the term 'crapper' is in memory of the Victorian English inventor, Thomas Crapper, who invented the modern flush toilet. It will come as no surprise to many that the most popular character for the last two years is Donald Trump!

Hot on the heels of the Belén is the Christmas Lottery, which is said to be the biggest of its kind in the world. Spanish people love to gamble, and the event on December 22 is a major event where many shops and businesses will close for a few hours to watch the event on television. If you walk down any shopping street on the morning of December 22nd, you will find that most shops are closed, and any people that are about will be crowded around a television screen or listening to a radio in one of the bars. The prizes are large, and there is said to be a one in seven chance of winning something. Listen out for the monotonous 'singing' from children announcing the winning numbers. I can guarantee that this noise will be difficult to get out of your head for at least a day afterwards!

Recognising that 5 January or Dia del Reys is of significant importance to most Spanish people, and in preference to Christmas Day, may take a little getting used to. Although Father Christmas or Santa Claus has become more popular in recent years, Christmas Eve (Nochebuena) is one of the big celebrations, with a big family gathering around a table full of treats and delicacies.

Christmas Day has only become commercially popular for gift giving in recent years. Instead, it remains a religious festival with attendance at midnight mass in church or cathedral, together with a family get together and a large meal.

January 5 is the day that you will see bakeries full of customers, desperate to buy their 'Roscón de Reyes´, which is a traditional ring-shaped cake, to be enjoyed on January 6th. Be careful when you eat a piece of this, as they contain a 'surprise' item that is prone to break teeth and give dentists an even happier and more prosperous New Year. Whoever discovers this 'gift' in their slice is crowned King or Queen. The downside, is that there is also a bean hidden in the cake; whoever finds this has to buy the roscón the following year.

January 6th is the traditional day when the Three Kings bring children their presents. In most villages, towns and cities, there will be a procession of the Three Kings, usually complete with camels, and onlookers are showered with sweets, which is when an upside-down umbrella may come in useful! The streets are full of loud music and celebration.

If you love April 1st, which is April Fool's Day in the UK, you will surely enjoy (or avoid) December 28th (Dia de los Santos Inocentes). This is the day for practical jokes, so be careful!

As in most countries, New Year's Eve is a big celebration in Spain. This is the event when partygoers are expected to eat 12 grapes quickly and drink a glass of cava at the stroke of midnight. One warning, do please be careful with the pips as there have been many unfortunate chocking incidents over the years. Basically, this 'tradition' was designed to clear an excess of grapes grown in Spain before they went off!

Speaking of choking, there are a few other things to get used to, such as turrón, which is a kind of nougat made from almonds, sugar and honey. Turrón is an acquired taste and for some, it can be a very sickly treat and is inclined to stick teeth together, which may come in useful in some circumstances over the Christmas holidays!

Looking back at Christmas past in the UK, it is certainly very different from the orange and nuts in my childhood Christmas stocking. The Christmas 'crappers' had yet to be invented, and colourful crackers complete with cheap hats and jokes on the Christmas dining table appear to be non-existent.

La Boda (The Wedding)

I gate-crashed a wedding last week. In my defence, it was a genuine accident, but I am rather pleased that I did. Like many people, I enjoy a good wedding; it is one of those events where the power of love forcibly overpowers the cynicism and doubt that can inhabit some of our lives. It takes the most hardened cynic not to feel just a twinge of emotion and 'something of the beyond' when watching a couple committing themselves to a life with each other.

I was enjoying a drink and people-watching in one of my favourite bars in a nearby village when a large crowd of chattering and laughing Canarians burst through the door. At first, I thought that it was a local fiesta, but all wore smart clothes and some were carrying small bouquets of flowers. I soon realised from the conversation that they were attending a wedding that was taking place in the small church next door to the bar. It always amuses me when I see bars situated very closely to the local church, but Catholic services to tend to go on for rather a long time, so I guess it is very sensible planning.

This particular group of wedding guests had arrived for the wedding service a little later than planned, and the small village church was already full. Undaunted, the group wisely decided to relocate to the bar next door and to begin their wedding celebrations early. I was told that both the bride and groom were very popular local teachers, which explained the large number of young people in the group.

Spanish and Canarians don't really do small intimate weddings; it is very much a case of 'the bigger the better', and it is not unusual to see the uninvited chatting and gossiping outside a church when the ceremony is in progress in the hope of catching a glimpse of the happy couple after the official event, and taking part in the celebrations afterwards. Spanish weddings are best regarded as marathons, and guests are well advised to allocate a whole day to the celebrations; they are best described as a test of endurance.

After throwing rice over the happy couple (confetti is just not done over here), the couple will be involved in endless photo shoots, which is a good time for guests to head to the local bar, often accompanied by the officiating priest. By the time that the real partying begins, guests are already very happy and ready to tuck into cocktails and canapes, followed by a multi-course banquet (sitting down, of course). Later, coffee and cake are served before guests head to the generous open bar and to enjoy the dancing and raunchy 'follow my leader' games that will eventually bring the celebrations to a close.

At this point, you may well be asking how all this partying is paid for. Traditionally, much of it is paid for by the guests, which is very much part of Spanish tradition going back to the days when this was the only way that a wedding could be paid for. If you are invited to a Spanish wedding, please don't think that presenting the happy couple with an electric toaster will get you off the hook. It will not, but a generous amount of cash or a cheque will do very nicely.

A basket is usually handed around during the reception to collect the generous monetary gifts, although the more discrete will have paid the money into the couple's bank account before the event. In order not to appear a cheapskate, a wedding gift should at least cover the cost of your food and drink at the reception, plus a bit more. My partying friends told me that 100 euros per person is currently regarded as the acceptable starting point.

My wedding party, and I say 'mine' because I was invited to join in, quickly entered into the celebratory spirit. Later, huge doors were opened to the rear of what appeared to be a small cafe bar to reveal a huge banqueting hall all beautifully set out for the lengthy banquet to come. We were soon joined by the main guests, looking very relieved as they escaped from the church and headed to the bar. Later, much later, the bride and groom would join the party and the real fun could begin.

I had unexpectedly witnessed and briefly taken part in yet another side of Canarian life. Sadly, I had another engagement to go to, and reluctantly left before the bride and groom returned from their photo shoot. I left wondering what condition the guests would be in the following morning, but felt quite sure that they would have given the happy couple a day that they would never forget.

For the Love of Paper

"The UK's National Health Service still relies on archaic fax machines" screamed the headlines this week. Oh well, I guess it makes a change from Brexit and Trump's controversial visit to the UK. Even so, I couldn't really see the problem, although I was supposed to be shocked when the article declared that a recent survey revealed that around 9000 fax machines are in use across England, with the Newcastle Upon Tyne Health Authority being the worst culprit with around 600 machines in daily use. Such horror!

I guess the reader was supposed to read between the lines that patients are at risk because of the use of this 'outdated technology', and of course the opportunity was used, as usual, to blame the funding crisis for 'the problem'. "This is ludicrous," screamed one senior surgeon, "The NHS cannot rely on technology that most other organisations scrapped in the early 2000s". Clearly, this esteemed surgeon has little knowledge of life in Spain, where the humble fax machine is still used and revered by most hospitals, surgeries, banks, local authorities and businesses.

When we moved to Spain, we were given several pieces of helpful advice from other expats. One of these pieces of advice was to "buy a fax machine" or at least to make sure that we had ready access to one. This piece of advice was invaluable and is still highly relevant. Over the last few months, I recall several occasions when I have been asked to fax a document to a bank, the customs office or local authority department. Indeed, my new mobile phone operator asked for a copy of my residency document to be faxed to them only the other day. Fax machines in Spain are still heavily used, valued and trusted. This is not to say that emailing documents is not possible, in most cases it is, but the Spanish have an ongoing love affair with paper and the fax machine fits the bill nicely.

The Spanish love affair with paper is to blame, of course. Despite the wonders of modern technology, the country still relies heavily upon paper records. I was recently persuaded to change my credit card, which I thought would be a simple process, since it was to be issued by the same bank branch that I have used for many years. The process was indeed simple, and all I had to do was to provide an electronic signature.

I made a comment to the bank clerk that this was so much easier than on previous occasions when I had left the bank with a handful of paper. He smiled knowingly and wandered over to his combined fax/printer, which was busily churning out continuous streams of paper. He gathered a handful and asked me to initial the fifteen pages before stamping each sheet with a momentary glint of pleasure and passing them to me. Hmm, so much for the use of technology I thought, as I left the bank clutching yet another handful of paper. Some things never change over here.

In Spain, the fax machine fits seamlessly into the love of paper that nothing else can replace. What can be more pleasurable that stuffing an important document into one machine and pressing a button, for it to appear out of another fax machine some distance away as if by magic. I have to admit that I also still enjoy the process and find it more reliable than battling with emails that may or may not be sent, or sorting out a computer virus, or whatever else should infect my laptop. A fax machine works, just as long as you load it up with paper and remember to top it up with ink and speak to it kindly. Yes, I know, it may jam occasionally, but we are not after perfection, are we?

Do I still use a fax machine? Well, yes and no. Our old fax machine died long ago and I now use an app on my smartphone that does the job nicely. However, I must admit that I do miss the physical process of sending and receiving a fax, knowing that it had been sent and receiving an automatic confirmation of receipt. What's not to like?

So, to those who bore us senseless about the 'digital revolution' and criticise the NHS for not scrapping their fax machines, I suggest the old adage that 'if it's not broke, don't fix it' may be relevant here. Many hospitals and GP surgeries may be quite content with this "outdated technology". Maybe it offers the security and reliability that emails, WhatsApp and Snapchat cannot provide. Oh, by the way, did I mention that the NHS is also being criticised for using that most antiquated of all technologies known as 'pagers'!

What's in a Name?

Now here's an essential question to start the day. Are you sufficiently worthy to have an airport named after you, and presumably after you die? Alternatively, if you don't consider that you meet these high specifications, do you know someone who does?

I have never been too sure about the wisdom of naming airports after people. If, for example, I wish to fly to Paris, I wish to fly to Paris and not into the arms of someone called Charles de Gaul. Why do airports in the United States have to be named after past Presidents? Washington National Airport used to be called just that until it was renamed the Ronald Reagan Airport; surely it was already named after a President called Washington, so I fail to see the point. In any case, just think of all those costs associated with new signs.

Despite some reservations, I was very pleased to hear that the island of Lanzarote will shortly be changing the name of its airport to Cesar Manrique. This name change has been requested by many residents for some time and was recently agreed by both the Prime Minister of Spain, Pedro Sanchez, and the President of the Canary Islands, Fernando Clavijo. As an admirer of the work of Cesar Manrique, I believe this to be an excellent choice in honouring someone who made a considerable and positive impact upon the island of Lanzarote, as well as the other islands in terms of architecture and the environment. Despite this endorsement, I am also well aware that there will be others who will see the change of airport name as controversial.

Other airport naming controversies include renaming the island of Madeira's airport to Cristiano Ronaldo International; I'm not too sure what the Spanish taxman thought of that particular honour. Anyone remember the footballer, George Best? In memory of both his on- and off-pitch antics, Belfast City Airport has become George Best Belfast City Airport; what a mouthful! Whether he is considered a footballing hero or not, many will be pleased to know that it has a rather good duty-free shop, which might be thought appropriate.

Over in Jamaica, I gather that the locals were not impressed when their airport was renamed after a part-time resident and author of novels about a British spy called James Bond. Many protested that the airport should have been named after a true islander, such as Usain Bolt, and not Ian Fleming.

John Lennon, Louis Armstrong, Mozart, Bill and Hilary Clinton, Marco Polo and even Robin Hood are all preserved for posterity in the names of some of the world's airports. Interestingly, the UK's Civil Aviation Authority has banned the official naming of British airports after famous people in the future, which I think is an excellent decision. Personally, I would much rather the airport be named after the place that I am travelling to rather than someone I have never heard of, or have no interest in. I am also very grateful that I am spared from flying to Margaret Thatcher International, but I guess whether or not you will agree will depend upon your own political point of view.

The Russia Connection

During the time that I have lived in the Canary Islands, I have come to understand, appreciate and admire the contribution and influence that these small islands have made over many years; an influence that is far in excess of the size of this unique archipelago.

Anyone who has travelled across these islands and has driven through some of the older road tunnels, carefully crafted through the centre of some of the volcanic mountains, will appreciate the impressive engineering skills demonstrated by the talented workers of earlier generations. I was reminded of this once again when it was reported that the authorities in St Petersburg, the second largest city in Russia, announced their decision to dedicate a bridge on the tributary of the Neva River in honour of the Canary Islands engineer, Agustín de Betancourt, who worked for Tsar Alexander I.

This bridge will be inaugurated on the eve of the opening of the World Cup later this year, which links the islands of Petroviski, Serni and Dekabristov through the Malaya Neva. The naming of this bridge after Agustín de Betancourt marks 260 years since the birth of this Tenerife engineer. This bridge will help to reduce the traffic congestion of St Petersburg, which has traffic jams as big as Moscow, and has a stadium that will host one of the World Cup semi-finals.

Agustín de Betancourt was born in 1758 in Puerto de la Cruz in Tenerife and his roots can be traced back to Jean de Béthencourt who began the colonisation of the Canary Islands in 1402, declaring himself as King of Tenerife in 1417. Agustin's father was a well-educated businessman with commercial interests in textile machinery, and his mother, Maria, was the first woman in Tenerife to publish a scientific article about dyes used in textiles. Agustin graduated in Madrid, and worked on canal buildings and mining, before travelling to Paris to study hydraulics and mechanics.

Betancourt had work published on engineering within the coal industry, but his main role was to discover new technologies that would benefit Spain. His work took him to England where he visited James Watt and Matthew Boulton, who were pioneers of the steam engine. Much of Betancourt's work appears to be connected with intelligence gathering from engineers working in France, England and the Netherlands, which would probably be called commercial espionage nowadays.

His interests were wide and varied ranging from the optical telegraph, Spain's first hot air balloon, harbour dredging, gun barrels, building a city jail, preservation of several ancient churches, building a cathedral and rebuilding a fairground, which gives a flavour of the interests and achievements of this dedicated engineer at work.

It was Betancourt who became the founder and director of the Institute of Communication Route Engineers, and, among other things, designed the first paper money printing machine in Tsarist Russia. He lived in Russia for 16 years and was also involved in construction projects in the Nizhny Novgorod main commercial precinct during the Nineteenth Century, and the modernisation of the Tula weapons factory. During his life, he also created the School of Civil Engineers of Roads, Canals and Ports for Madrid and built the Double Effect Steam Machine.

Agustín de Betancourt died in 1824 in St Petersburg. Engineer, architect, builder and inventor, Agustin de Betancourt has a memorial in the form of a bust in the premises of the University of Railway Engineering and is buried in the cemetery of Alexandr Nevsky Monastery in St Petersburg. Once again, many will be surprised, as well as humbled, by the achievements of this son of the Canary Islands.

Staying Healthy

The Canary Islander

Overweight 'Bridegrooms of Death'

I guess that many of us may have over indulged during the Christmas and New Year festivities, and I assume that many are now in the period where reluctant gym memberships are booming, as well as desperate subscriptions to Weight Watchers. Sadly, all those temptations do have a price to pay when we see that we can no longer squeeze into our favourite clothes.

One of the many fat inducing temptations readily available in Spain and the Canary Islands are 'Churros con Chocolate', which is basically deep-fried pastry strips, rolled in sugar and dipped into hot chocolate as they are eaten. This 'snack' is hugely popular in Spain, Portugal and the Canary Islands, as well as the United States, France and Mexico.

Depending upon the time of day, and the state of your appetite, they can be both delicious and disgusting at the same time. Indeed, it is not unusual to see locals polishing off a huge quantity of churros in cafe bars for their breakfast. Needless to say, it is an excellent way to pile on the pounds, as well as keeping the health service busy with the coronaries that are the result of this over indulgence. My advice is to avoid them at all costs.

Speaking of being overweight and diets, you really should take a look at Spain's 'Bridegrooms of Death', which is the cheerful nickname given to Spain's elite infantry regiment, 'La Legión'. The regiment is loosely based upon the French Foreign Legion, as a prestige combat unit with its best-known member being General Franco during the Spanish Civil War.

Usually admired for their handsome physical appearance, these fine men are usually well known for their tasselled caps, to keep the flies off, and open necked shirts, to keep the ladies interested. Their uniform traditionally does not have a top button, which aids their reputation as "the top totty killers of Europe". Sadly, this much-coveted reputation is rapidly disappearing, since it was found that a significant percentage of the 3000 troops were found to be obese, based upon their body mass index (BMI) of over 30.

This elite force is now having a few problems in the obesity department and the troops are now being given dietary advice, nutrition tips, as well as additional exercise to overcome their rapidly expanding waistlines with a target loss of between 500g and 1kg a week. Although 'La Legión makes the valid point that significant weight gain may be as a result of cultural, pathological and psychological factors, I firmly believe that churros and hot chocolate are to blame.

So, there we have it. As we humbly trot off to the gym at the beginning of this New Year, and preferably to one that does not include a bar and restaurant, let us think long and hard about these fine Spanish men who are undertaking one of the biggest battles of their lives - that of losing weight without the comfort of a plateful of churros and hot chocolate to fall back on. Sadly, for many, I suspect that it will soon not just be the top button of their shirt that is missing.

Kill or Cure?

An article about bee sting therapy caught my eye this week. Tragically, a woman recently died in Spain after undergoing a bizarre form of therapy at a clinic that involved bee venom. The therapy is known as apitherapy, which involved the woman attending a session every four weeks for two years, which was designed to improve her muscular control without allergic reactions.

As a child, and as unlikely as it now seems, I remember attempting handstands on the lawn of our garden. Unfortunately, during this challenging activity, I placed my hand over a bee who was sunning himself quietly in the grass. The bee quickly let it be known that he was not happy with my gymnastic efforts. I remember that the resulting sting was very painful and that my mother quickly removed the sting once she had realised what all the fuss was about. I also recall taking great consolation after I was told that a bee can only sting once, and then it dies.

Several weeks later, I remember my father coming home from work, telling us that the young wife of a good friend and colleague had died from a bee sting that very morning. I remember my parents being very upset about this tragedy, and after my event a few weeks earlier, I considered myself to be extremely fortunate, given the circumstances. Since that time, I have always treated bees with the utmost respect and until recently have had a somewhat cynical view of how bee stings can actually help to preserve and enhance life; I am now having some doubts.

Bee Sting Therapy claims to bring relief and healing for spinal, neural, joint and musculoskeletal conditions that includes gout, arthritis, tendinitis, shingles, Parkinson's Disease, Alzheimer's, cancerous tumours, fibromyalgia, cramps, pulled muscles and many other ailments. The therapy is based upon the idea that bee venom stimulates the adrenal glands after a sting, which produces the hormone, cortisol, which has anti-inflammatory properties that jump starts the healing process.

This is not as unlikely as it sounds, since it has been reported for some time that venom from bees, as well as snakes, spiders, scorpions and sea urchins have the potential to work as the next generation of drugs that have the ability to effectively fight cancer. Needless to say, pharmaceutical companies are currently working hard to exploit the potential of these natural remedies to enhance their balance sheets and to impress their shareholders. The theory is impressive and I hope that current research bears positive results that will improve the lives of so many people suffering from a range of debilitating and life-threatening conditions.

This particular therapy involves holding a bee by its head and pinching it until the bee's stinger emerges and punctures the patient's skin. Sadly, the poor bee always dies in the process, since they can only use their sting once. In the case of the patient in Spain; she suffered an anaphylactic shock, developed wheezing and lost consciousness. An ambulance was called, a steroid was administered, but no adrenaline was made available. The bee sting had triggered a stroke, the patient fell into a permanent coma, and sadly died a few weeks later from multi organ failure.

Advocates of apitherapy make many claims for its health benefits, which remain largely unsupported by traditional medicine, but such cynicism has been faced by advocates of chiropractic, acupuncture and aromatherapy, amongst other therapies. Indeed, some therapies, previously regarded as 'fringe' by the established medical profession, have gained a reputation as effective therapies in recent years and are often used to support traditional medicine. This sad incident in Spain is reportedly the first case of death by bee venom. I will continue to do my best to keep an open mind about this and other therapies, but at the moment would prefer that my only contact with bees is through honey on my morning toast.

All Helmets and Lycra

Over the years, cyclists from all over Europe have headed to the Canary Islands to take advantage of some decent weather with which to indulge in their favourite pastime. All of the inhabited islands have become increasingly popular, but with the favourite destinations being Tenerife, Gran Canaria, Lanzarote and Fuerteventura that are selected as ideal destinations for all-year-round cycling. The tourist boards and hotels are grateful, since income from cyclists and their entourages makes a healthy contribution to tourist income.

As well as heat, the islands offer mountains, breath-taking scenery and a refreshing sea breeze. Rainfall is rare during most of the year, which makes the islands ideal for winter training. The main disadvantage are the dust storms, which although occasional, are like riding through a blanket of hot, dry fog. These 'calimas' are caused by very fine sand being blown from the Sahara.

Locals are wise enough to know that they should remain indoors in such conditions, but it is not unusual to see dozens of cyclists attempting to complete their training schedule in conditions that must be injurious to their general health, and with some being admitted to hospital for treatment. Those suffering from asthma, as well as other breathing conditions, would do well to avoid cycling on the islands during the presence of a calima.

Whilst following behind two 'team cyclists' the other day, who incidentally were holding hands, it occurred to me that I rarely see a happy cyclist nowadays. They all seem to be so deadly serious, gritting their teeth and with huge quantities of sweat leaking from their designer Lycra. It looks to be anything but pleasurable and seems to be more of a test of endurance; maybe that is the point. I rarely see cyclists actually enjoying their cycling in the beautiful scenery that these islands have to offer. Their eyes seem to be glued to the road just ahead of them, or glued to the sensuous bottom of the team cyclist in front.

It all seems such hard work nowadays; whatever happened to cycling for fun? Am I the only one who remembers actually enjoying cycling to work or going for a leisurely cycle in the countryside with friends, and stopping for a pub lunch before cycling home? Cyclists visiting these islands have spent a considerable amount of money on flights and accommodation, as well as transporting their cycles from their home countries, so why waste it peddling aimlessly up and down the same stretch of road near my home?

As I cautiously follow the two cyclists holding hands, musing on my cycling memories from the past, other motorists were getting impatient behind me. Road conditions meant that I could not overtake, so I was content to wait. However, others were not, which encouraged one very angry motorist to hoot the cyclists loudly, as he overtook me whilst approaching a bend. The cycling 'lovebirds' merely dropped their physical connection briefly and offered the angry motorist a one-finger salute, which is not the best way to gain friends or to promote one's sport.

Anger is never appropriate in these circumstances, but it did remind me of a number of emails that I have received in recent months, complaining that "cyclists are a nuisance" (with much stronger language being used). It is also clear that negative comments on the islands' social media are rapidly increasing, with angry comments declaring that team cyclists are becoming a curse on the islands' roads. Rarely does a week pass without at least one cyclist being seriously injured during a road traffic accident, or even worse, alongside their crushed cycle. There are regular reports of children, the elderly, the infirm and those simply not paying attention, being hit by a speeding cyclist. It seems that the days of welcoming team cyclists to these islands is fast disappearing.

The old adage of 'each to their own' comes to mind, but maybe enjoyment from cycling can be achieved without inconveniencing, annoying or maiming pedestrians and other road users. An appropriate message to team cyclists might be to enjoy these beautiful islands, appreciate the ever-changing scenery, adjust appropriately to road conditions, and to be thoughtful towards others. Maybe looking less desperate and smiling a little, might help too? Speed and sweat is not what life in the Canary Islands is about.

An Appointment for an Appointment

I really don't like August! It is not the excessive heat and accompanying high electricity bills for air conditioning that upset me, but the fact that nearly everyone seems to be on holiday. No, I do not begrudge hard working Spanish and Canarians some precious time off with their families, but the concept of holiday cover has never been invented in Spain. Post is rarely delivered during August, since our postman is climbing a mountain somewhere; we have learned never to order anything that needs delivering in August. Similarly, we try to avoid anything involving the bank, social security office, Town Hall or health centre that requires anything needing filling in, bonking with a rubber stamp or using the computer.

Over the years, we have learned the hard way, but sometimes things just crop up and have to be dealt with. The lack of holiday cover means that if someone is away at the bank or Town Hall, then that is just tough luck; you will have to wait until they return in September. Even the computers are on holiday in August and refuse to work until the temperature cools down ...

It all came to a head this morning when I tried to replace a health card with one of the newly issued ones, for reasons that seem neither logical or sensible. I don't usually fret too much about such changes, since when there is a change of government, health and other cards are often suddenly cancelled without due notice, but with Brexit approaching, one has to be prepared.

I came across a newly invented phenomenon this week, which is the necessity to make an appointment in order to get an appointment at the health centre. This is the latest ploy to put off actually seeing anyone in August and (temporarily) does away with the need to employ additional staff. Mind you, the system falls to pieces a few weeks later, but I guess the hope is that patients will either have died, recovered or left the country, so I guess there is a form of logic in operation, which brings me nicely to the case of the woman with a leg attached to a broom handle.

Did you know that computers also suffer from the August holiday syndrome, and try to take some time off? I overheard a woman being told that she would have to return later in the week because the computers had slowed down due to the excessive heat in the office. Now this was no ordinary case, since the poor soul had one leg strapped to what looked like a broom handle; clearly, she was in some discomfort. The woman took it all in good part, nodded, and limped away. She had made the effort get to the health centre to make an appointment in order to get an appointment to book an appointment with a specialist… Now back to my replacement health card.

Since the wait for a real, plastic health card could well exceed the lifetime of many patients, the health centre has come up with a jolly good wheeze, which is to issue a temporary one on a sheet of paper; that is if both the computer and printer are working. In my case, both were having an August holiday and I was asked to return another day. Oh well, it is no more than I would expect.

Over the years as an expat living in Spain, I have got used to what I see as the quirkiness and sheer inefficiencies of many of the bureaucratic processes that this country copes with. If something isn't working, the response is usually to invent something that will make it even worse and to employ more civil servants in the process. I have learned, as have many expats, to balance these minor irritations with the joys and advantages of other aspects of my life in Spain, so I usually grit my teeth and try to avoid thinking too much like a Brit.

I often try to explain and defend Spanish systems and lengthy bureaucratic processes to other expats on the basis that maybe they didn't fully understand the language during their latest bureaucratic encounters, or maybe it is down to cultural differences and misunderstandings about the way that things are done. I am sure that if you ask a German or Polish expat trying to navigate the paperwork processes in the UK they would tell of similar experiences.

Did I get my new temporary health card? Well, yes and no. During a return visit to the health centre, by means of an appointment to get an appointment, I finally arrived once again to face the offending computer and printer. This time, both were having a good day and eventually spewed out the required document. The lady at the desk was also looking less flustered than when she had dealt with the leg woman, and kindly suggested that it would be a good idea to have the document laminated, since it may be many years before my real card arrived in the post. I took her advice, thanked her and headed to my local print shop.

At the print shop, the laminating machine was also having an August day. It greedily gobbled up my card, but refused to release it from the other end of the machine. There was a smell of burning and flames appeared from the centre of the laminating machine. After the fire was put out, the now worried looking operator got a screwdriver and gingerly opened the blackened machine. Inside were the charred remains of my new temporary health card. Ah well, such is life in August; I will return to the office to make an appointment for an appointment tomorrow and then we will start the game all over again.

In the end, I did manage to collect my new, shiny health card from a very helpful lady operating from a small, airless room marked 'Resuscitation'. I now know why!

Avoid the Doctor, Eat Honey

We will soon be heading into the season of coughs, colds and flu once again, together with the misery that such conditions bring. In most cases, these illnesses are relatively short-lived, but can be unpleasant, inconvenient and annoying, and also serious in cases where there are underlying health conditions.

Coughs are mostly caused by a cold or flu virus, or bronchitis, and will usually last for around three weeks. Antibiotics make very little difference to symptoms and can have unpleasant side-effects. More importantly, unnecessary prescriptions reduce their effectiveness. As a child, whenever I had a cough or cold, the first thing that my mother would do was to give me a regular concoction of blackcurrant juice and honey to drink. It was a very comforting drink and certainly helped to reduce symptoms.

In adult life, I continue to follow this advice, although with the addition of a large tot of whisky for good measure. It is honey that is the magic ingredient, because it is a natural antibiotic. Doctors in the UK are now asking their patients to eat honey before visiting their local surgery if they have a cough or cold. It is all part of a growing effort to tackle the problem of resistance to antibiotics. Of course, to benefit from honey we must also have bees.

In recent years, there has been considerable hybridisation of bee species with the importation of bees to the Canary Islands that were supposed to be more productive. The native Canary Black Bee is now officially declared to be a breed in danger of extinction. It was only on the small Canary Island of La Palma that pure populations were discovered, and in 2001 a law to conserve the Canary Black Bee population was introduced, and the introduction of foreign subspecies was banned.

There are now at least 500 colonies of the Canary Black Bee on the island, which are resistant to many diseases that many bees succumb to. This native bee has very specific characteristics that make it highly productive, gentle and is unlikely to attack others. In Gran Canaria, the Government recently announced that they too were not only going to give special protection to the Canary Black Bee, but to ensure its distinctive survival by selecting a group of island beekeepers who will help to ensure that its genetic purity lives on.

Bees are very important for our very survival; the simple headline fact is that if bees didn't exist, neither would humans. Bees are responsible for much of the food that we eat, since they keep plants and crops alive. One surprising fact is that around one third of the food that we eat is pollinated by bees. Bees do not pollinate our crops out of a sense of duty to the human race; they simply eat to survive. They absorb the protein that they need from pollen and all of the carbohydrates that they need from nectar. Bees feed from flowers, and as they move from flower to flower they just happen to provide an essential service to humans.

Pesticides appear be the main cause of the problem, although some experts also attribute some of the collapse of the bee population to climate change, the loss of their usual habitat and attacks from a variety of parasites.

Popular pesticides known as neonicotinoids, which is similar to nicotine, cause bees to go insane and to abandon their hives; they don't know how to return home and some experts claim that they develop a form of Alzheimer's. Maybe this disturbing link with nicotine-based products that attack bees should give a serious warning to human smokers too.

Climate change also can take its fair share of blame with the disruption of the natural synchronisation of bee hibernation and flower opening, which causes bees to die. Despite this gloomy scenario, some positive steps are being made to help to rebuild and sustain bee populations. Measures to address the problem are being taken in a number of countries. Strategies include funding to help farmers to establish new habitats for bee populations, alternatives to nicotine-based pesticides, as well as support from bee keepers, such as those in La Palma and Gran Canaria who are determined to maintain the viability of the species.

In order to prepare for the forthcoming season of coughs and colds, do take my mother's advice and remember to include a jar of Canarian honey in your shopping basket. It is not only delicious, but it really does help.

Sunbeds R Us

I am often told that Brits on holiday like nothing better than to get out of bed long before their all-inclusive breakfast has even hit the frying pan, and to chase outside to the swimming pool in their boxer shorts or bras (or possibly both) in order to place a vivid Union flag towel on the sunbed of their choice. It is even more exciting if there is a mad competitive dash with the Germans, with Brits gaining immense satisfaction if they reach their prized position first.

Why, oh why is one of the tour companies determined to ruin such jingoistic pleasures with the introduction of a 'book and pay before you arrive' sunbed option when booking a holiday in the Canary Islands. For the princely sum of 22 euros per person per week, potential holidaymakers can view a virtual image of their choice of sunbed, together with its ideal position close to the swimming pool, bar or most importantly, the toilets, from their home in Mansfield before even stepping on the plane.

Gone are those heady days of the mad dash before breakfast. One thing to be thankful for, I guess, is that Ryanair will not be in charge of the seating allocations. Just imagine it, the entire family split up and lost in various dark corners of the pool area. Oh yes, I nearly forget to mention, the only reason for this change of sunbed policy is to raise additional cash for the tour operators. After all, their senior executives are anticipating a hefty pay increase on the back of it, and an additional charge of £176 for a family of four staying for two weeks is not to be sneezed at. Maybe now they can also employ someone to give the sunbeds a good scrub down from time to time?

Spoilsports or what? Personally, I have little time for sunbeds mainly because of the dubious sticky residue that is often lingering after the visit of the previous guest. I also get bored very easily, and lying on a sunbed for more than 30 minutes is not my idea of a good time. Would I select a sunbed close to a swimming pool anyway? Certainly not. As someone who has spent a good part of an earlier career looking after a primary school swimming pool, I know only too well what goes into them, and it has very little to do with pre-packaged chemicals. I shall never forget that heady perfume of a mixture of chlorine and urine and, as a result, I now do my utmost to avoid swimming pools of any kind.

I also have a problem with Madge and her family. Remember that television series, Benidorm? Whenever I see a sunbed, I have a vision of that foul speaking creature, Madge, and her apology of a family, all desperately trying to achieve the impossible by gaining both the skin of an elephant and an untreatable form of skin cancer in just one week's holiday in the sun. Just add a mobility scooter and we could create our own series right here in the Canary Islands.

I guess that I should now mention Brexit, but only in very hushed tones, of course, since people can be very sensitive about such comments. I hear that the Germans have had this option of pre-booking a sunbed for many years. You really must hand it to them - first class organisers, as well as VWs and sausage.

Now for the bad news; rumour has it that the new 'book a sunbed before you fly' option will only be available until Britain leaves the European Union. After that, it will be a point of serious negotiation and strategic compromise, but my sources in Brussels tell me that the likelihood of maintaining this advantage will be dependent upon a satisfactory trade deal. I guess that Mrs May will have a problem with this one, and I expect she will be looking for a lengthy transition period.

Reliable sources close to the centre of UK decision making also tell me that the Honourable Member of Parliament for the 18th Century, Joseph Septimus Smog, is determined that this newly acquired right of expat sunbed reservation will never be taken away, and certainly never given up to the Germans. Indeed, he has staked his future and that of his unborn child, Octavius Smog, on this one. Let's wait and see.

So, to British holidaymakers everywhere, do make the most of the new sense of freedom that this new sunbed strategy will give you, even if only for a short time. That dash outside in the early hours of the morning, to casually throw a Union flag towel over your choice of sunbed with gay abandon could shortly be a thing of the past. Brits can now awake at a sensible time and enjoy their all-inclusive breakfast in peace.

An Elderly Expat Dog

One of the fine qualities that I greatly admire in British and other expats living in Spain, is their willingness to share their home with a stray dog or cat. Many newly arrived expats quickly recognise the plight of stray and unwanted animals in Spain. Unlike the UK, there are few animal shelters and animal welfare charities dedicated to caring for and rehoming unwanted dogs and cats. Over the years, the situation has improved, thanks in many ways to the dedication of expats who have taken it upon themselves to establish charities and to raise funds to support rehoming and education projects.

For us, a bedraggled puppy that looked much like a fruit bat, burst into our lives fourteen years ago, following an announcement on a radio programme that I was involved in whilst working in the Costa Blanca. Bella, as she was named, quickly became a much-loved part of our family, sharing her new home with our loveable, yet stubborn corgi, Barney, and later with Mac, a house cat, who sat firmly at the top of the family chain of command. Over the years, Bella has become an intrinsic part of our expat adventure and now lives with us in the Canary Islands.

We are often told that, if we are fortunate, we live longer than our ancestors, which is why the age of retirement has been extended and why we are all now expected to work longer. However, with advancing years comes the health problems associated with ageing that our ancestors did not share. It is the same for animals too, and this is the stage that Bella has now entered. For many years, Bella has been a fit, healthy and lively dog, visiting the vet each year for her annual check-up and vaccinations. Over recent years, we have modified her diet to accommodate the ageing process. Last year, Bella lost her hearing, which did not seem to trouble her unduly. Although she could no longer respond to our voice commands, her sense of smell rapidly improved. Instead of listening and responding to voice commands, Bella simply followed our hand signals and seemed to sense what we wanted her to do.

Several weeks ago, we noticed that Bella's sight was also failing. She occasionally fell off the edge of a pavement when she was out for a walk or she would walk into a plant or a post. Inside the house, she behaved normally, even running up and down stairs without any problem at all. Our vet advised us to take Bella to a specialist, since the surgery was not equipped to deal with major eye issues and suggested that we take Bella to see a consultant at the University Veterinary Hospital, which is where vets are trained.

The veterinary hospital will only see animals that have been referred to them by local vets, and they offer a limited number of appointments. Bella was seen by an ophthalmic specialist, accompanied by a number of final year veterinary students. It was impressive to listen to the clear diagnosis of Bella's condition by the specialist and the depth of questioning and treatment suggestions from the final year students. As well as a thorough eye examination, Bella had an echogram, during which it was found that much of Bella's condition was age related. However, an ulcer was found on her eye, which was causing her discomfort, and might require surgery. Due to Bella's advancing years, this was the least preferred option.

Over a period of the next four weeks, we administered antibiotics and pain relief drops into Bella's eyes four times a day, as well as encouraging her to drink liquid medicine. This was not an easy process, which we dreaded as much as Bella. The snarling and growling when administering drops indicated just a little of the discomfort and anger that Bella was so forcibly expressing.

Each time we returned to the veterinary hospital, there was an improvement. The specialist finally confirmed that the ulcer had healed and that Bella was no longer in any pain and would not require surgery. It was a huge relief and we are grateful for the care and specialist support that Bella has received. Sadly, Bella has lost nearly all of her eyesight with just a little peripheral vision remaining. However, as I write this, she is soundly asleep and snoring. Bella continues to be interested in all that is going on; she enjoys her food and eats well. She still plays with some of her toys and enjoys a very short walk on a lead. Although we know that our time with Bella is limited, we are certainly going to make the most of the time that we have left with her.

Life and Death

Don't Shoot the Messenger!

It has been amusing to read comments about the islands' weather in the press and social media over the last few days. Apparently, the Canary Islands have only just survived storm and tempest and all manner of tragedy. Flights have been cancelled, airports destroyed, cars and roads have been washed away and, basically all hell has broken loose on these 'Paradise Islands'. According to the Mail, Sun and Express, life as we know it on these islands is about to come to an end. Hmm, really?

Fear not, the sun is out again today, and apart from a few more potholes in the roads, and some vigorous mopping of patios, life is more or less back to normal. It has been a bit wet, of course; some flights have been delayed for a few hours, but life continues in much the same way as it did before the rain. These islands do get quite a lot of rain each February, which is why flights and accommodation are usually cheaper than at other times of the year, and some years are worse than others.

In short, there is nothing to get too alarmed about, but the tabloid press is having a field day about "Tourism Disaster in the Canary Islands". Maybe they are talking about life in an alternative universe, or did they simply exaggerate a minor inconvenience to sell a few more copies?

Brits love to talk, and preferably complain, about the weather. Conversely, most Canarians that I speak to have welcomed the refreshing rain that has cleansed our streets from the dust and sandstorms (and dog poo) that have lingered from the summer months. The reservoirs, which were almost empty and were the subject of alternative 'doomsday' scenarios in the popular press, have been replenished and the islands' forests and green spaces are actually rapidly changing from a dusty brown to a lovely fresh green once again. Everything smells so fresh and new again; what's not to like?

Those reporting sensationalist stories and posting heavily doctored videos about the islands' weather forget that few homes in the Canary Islands have the benefit of gutters, roadside drains, and even a damp-proof course within the basic infrastructure to deal with an excessive fall of rain; we don't usually need it. As a result, we do get a few problems from time to time, but it is hardly the stuff to get too stressed about. In true Canarian tradition, all is well after two or three days and any inconveniences are quickly forgotten.

For many holidaymakers, of course, the Canary Islands are the subject of dreams and heightened anticipation for a forthcoming holiday in the sun. It also costs a lot of money to get away for a few days, and who wants their dreams to be shattered? How dare anyone publish anything that detracts from this view of 'Paradise Islands'. Indeed, I have read a number of comments from both residents and holidaymakers complaining that the local press should not be writing anything negative about the weather, because it is bound to have a negative impact upon the tourist industry. Fine, let's just publish fake news, and forget all about reporting reality. Is that what tourists really want?

The truth that is often ignored is that these islands are not always the 'Paradise' that is usually portrayed by the tourist industry. We have our fair share of crime with murders, theft, stabbings, drownings, drug and alcohol abuse, prostitution, and partner, child and animal abuse are all reported in our weekly news. We boast of more drownings on these islands than any other region of Spain. The islands suffer from poverty, homelessness, require food banks, and face huge unemployment, as well as being the most unpopular region in all of Spain for the quality of employment opportunities.

There, we have it; these islands are not always 'Paradise' that many like to claim they are, but are merely a romantic illusion of an idealistic world, which may help to fulfil fantasies during a couple of weeks' holiday in the sun. If you think about it, they cannot be anything else; after all, flawed human beings live and work on these islands, therefore nothing can be perfect.

For much of the year, the sun shines, and tourists come and go. Many arrive pale and sick; some with colds, flu, depression and anxiety in a bid to forget their troubles, albeit briefly. For most holidaymakers, these islands help to refresh and replenish the soul, give inspiration, relaxation and much needed rest to troubled minds. For most of the year, they do a pretty good job, but let us also remember that these islands have their 'off days' too.

The Cost of Expats Dying

With the exception of articles about receiving British television in Spain, the most popular article on my 'Living in Spain and the Canary Islands' website continues to be 'Death in Spain', which is why I repeat the publication of this article from time to time. Death is a subject that no one really wants to talk about, but most wise expats know that they should give it some thought, if only to spare their loved ones' unnecessary problems during a distressing time.

I came face to face with this issue several years ago following the death of a good friend living in Spain. Peter had no living relatives either in Spain or in the UK, and it was left to local friends to ensure that his wishes were carried out. Peter had willed his body for medical research, but because he died of cancer, the body was rejected by the research institute. Peter had expressed no other wishes, and his friends therefore decided that cremation would be the next best alternative.

Meanwhile, Peter's body was resting in a makeshift mortuary in a private hospital, which sadly also doubled up as a laundry and storage room, with open doors to the car park outside the building. It was imperative that the body be moved as a matter of urgency, because of the heat of the summer. It is not due to lack of sensitivity, but for good reason, that most bodies are either cremated or buried within two or three days of death in most parts of Spain and the Canary Islands.

Calls to the funeral directors revealed that they would require a deposit of around 4000 euros before they would even remove the body from the hospital. By that time, Peter's bank accounts had already been frozen, and it was unlikely that there were sufficient funds available in the account anyway. It was up to Peter's friends to collect the funds necessary to pay the undertakers before the body could be moved. Eventually, the deposit was paid, and the funeral company removed the body from the hospital; the funeral and cremation could then go ahead.

As a friend witnessing these events during a distressing period, it made me realise that everyone, and certainly all expats, should make provision for their passing to avoid unnecessary distress and burdens placed upon those that are left. Although it was always something that I had intended to do, this experience made me visit a Spanish insurance company that had been highly recommended a few days after the funeral. For a very modest monthly premium, both my partner and myself are now fully covered - nothing too fancy, just a dignified, and hopefully efficient, end of a story.

Although I am not going to make any recommendations as to the best companies to insure with, I would urge all expats to take out some kind of cover, unless wealthy enough to have a substantial reserve of cash that is readily available to the next of kin. Readily available is the key phrase here, since bank accounts in Spain are rapidly frozen upon death, which can make access to funds difficult at a time when it is most needed.

There are currently many insurance companies advertising funeral plans to expats, with some requiring substantial payments up front. Realising that there is a ready market in expat death, headlines such as "Funeral Costs Rising at a Shocking Rate", and depressing graphs showing "The Cost of Dying" are currently appearing in many online publications. Of course, these advertisements are meant to frighten as well as to inform, but they do have a useful function in alerting expats to potential problems that they may face.

Experience tells me that whilst some may prefer to pay the full cost of their funeral up front, it is not necessary, and good, basic cover is available for a reasonable monthly or annual premium. For me, a Spanish insurance company with a good track record, together with recommendations from friends was the best choice. As with most of the larger purchases in life, carefully shop around for the best prices and ask questions before you commit yourself.

Ashes to Ashes

I received a very moving email from a regular 'Letters from the Atlantic' reader and correspondent this week. Janice lives in the UK and has been a regular visitor to the Canary Islands over the last 47 years with her husband, Bob. Sadly, Bob died a few weeks ago, shortly after their 47th wedding anniversary, which they celebrated on their favourite Canary Island. Janice and Bob had visited the same island each year since their honeymoon, and in the same fishing village, which they both loved. The couple were true Canary Island lovers and there was only one year that they did not manage a visit, which was shortly after the birth of their son.

Janice told me that Bob had cancer, and it was during their last visit to the island that he had commented in his favourite restaurant that he would like to have his ashes scattered in the sea from the Canarian village that they had visited and enjoyed so much. Bob had remarked that it would be rather like "coming home". In her email to me, Janice asked if scattering ashes was allowed, since she had read that it was forbidden to scatter human remains in the Canary Islands.

Janice is correct, since it is illegal to scatter ashes on land or sea without obtaining a special licence, yet getting a licence remains a mystery. My enquiries on behalf of Janice at several town halls on the larger islands have led nowhere, so if anyone has further information about the procedure, do please let me know.

There is a potential fine of around 2000 euros if caught scattering human ashes in public places. Despite this restriction, I do know that one of the islands, Tenerife, has a 'Garden of Ashes' in La Laguna where ashes can be scattered without a fee, but this facility does not exist on all the islands.

My best advice to Janice is for her to make enquiries with local funeral directors on the island. The other, slightly riskier, alternative is to ask a local fisherman in the village to sail well out of the harbour area and to discretely scatter the ashes whilst out at sea. Surely this can be no worse than some of the pollution that regularly finds its way into the sea?

I know from personal experience that scattering ashes is not always an easy thing to do on these islands, since by their very nature these islands can be very windy and 'ash blowback' from a traditional urn can be a highly distressing experience. The best approach is to ask the funeral director to provide a plastic tube that is designed both for plane transportation, as well as for scattering the remains of a loved one, which Janice and her son are planning shortly.

Readers may like to know that human ashes can be carried on an aircraft, although a plastic container should be requested from the funeral director to allow for the container to be easily scanned by airport security.

Although the ashes can be checked in as cargo inside suitcases, it is probably better to include them as part of hand luggage. Do ensure that airport check-in staff know that human remains are being carried. The death certificate of the deceased should also be available, together with any other information given by the funeral director.

Losing a loved one is always a distressing affair, but it can be made easier in the knowledge that we have done our best to meet their wishes. Let us hope that Janice and her son take some comfort by revisiting a place that she and Bob loved so much by "Coming home".

Communicating with Beer and Stones

"Do You Speak English?"

I wonder if anyone made a New Year's resolution to learn a new language? I admire any expats who make a determined effort to learn the language of their host country and are willing to try to avoid asking that embarrassing question "Do you speak English?" at every opportunity. After all, without a basic knowledge of the language, culture and customs, much of the new life that was hoped for will never be achieved. No, I am not talking about not seeking translation support when dealing with medical, legal and financial matters, where it is often important to seek professional assistance. I won't pretend that learning a language is easy as one gets older; it is not, since learning a new language takes perseverance and effort.

I was pleased to read in the papers this week that both Prince George and his sister, Princess Charlotte, are learning Spanish at their young age. They do have one major advantage, of course, in that their nanny is Spanish. As well as an acceptance of the need to reach out to a wider world, the appreciation, skill and some proficiency in communicating in another language will help these young people to recognise that they do not live in a solely English-speaking world and will help to give them a wider perspective of countries and cultures outside the United Kingdom.

During my time as a school inspector working in Wales, as well as England, I was always pleased to meet many young children who were confident in speaking both Welsh and English. The very act of learning a second language at such a young age makes the brain more receptive to the learning of other languages later in their school life. I recall detailed research reports that indicated that children learning both Welsh and English achieved far higher success rates when it came to learning other languages than their English counterparts. The message is clear; to be a successful linguist, it is important that youngsters start learning a second language, any language, early in life.

I often hear from would-be expats who wisely make a determined effort to learn the language for some years before they even attempt to move to Spain. Others arrive in Spain and suddenly realise, and panic after a few brusque encounters at the Town Hall, that some grasp of the language would be useful. It is at this stage that those long forgotten Linguaphone tapes suddenly see daylight after many years. Sometimes, newly arrived expats find themselves attending over-crowded language classes provided by the Town Hall, whilst others seek private lessons or attend a 'crash course'. Whatever the approach, a recognition that not everyone in the world speaks English is a good start.

Many teachers of Spanish will confidently assure expats arriving in Spain that anyone over the age of 50 can successfully learn the language. I question this assertion as basically a ploy to gain more generous fee-paying students, although I am sure that many will contradict me. Let's be honest, most older people find that learning a new language later in life to be challenging, but certainly not impossible. Whatever the result, the effort is always appreciated by the locals, and the ability to speak a few sentences, and to understand what is going on is invaluable when starting a new life in Spain, or any other country for that matter.

Many experts maintain that a grasp of English, Spanish and Chinese is all that is needed to conquer the linguistic world. I believe this to be true, since Spanish is the second most used language in the world after English. It always pleases me when I hear that Spanish is being taught in British schools, since I have always believed that this is the natural second language, and considerably more useful than French in today's world. No, I am not a great enthusiast for the teaching of French in British schools, but it is certainly better than nothing at all.

I was once told that the best way for expats to learn a new language is to have an affair with a new partner from the country of your choice. Now, I am not suggesting that expats go in for partner swapping, but the point is that for learning to be successful, it requires a thorough immersion in the culture and traditions of the country, and not only learning the language as a dry academic exercise.

Learn a Language with Beer and Insomnia

Those expats who enjoy a tipple will no doubt be delighted to read the news that I am reporting this week. According to researchers, German students studying the Dutch language found that their pronunciation improved remarkably after drinking just one pint of beer each. So, I guess many readers are now wondering if a glass or two of Spanish Rioja before attempting to speak Spanish might be of help? Sadly, I have no more information about this, but if you too find that your Spanish language skills soar following a few drinks, do please let me know and I will pass this information on to the researchers.

As far as more traditional approaches are concerned, I remember a brief period as an awkward teenager when I suddenly decided to learn Russian, which I now confess was designed mainly to annoy my parents. I invested in a small pillow speaker linked to a tape recorder that was supposed to help me to learn the new vocabulary whilst I slept. Sadly, during one restless night I became so entangled in the cables that it destroyed the connection and damaged the tape recorder; my confidence in this new approach to learning was badly shaken. It was an experiment without a satisfactory conclusion.

A more serious study has recently found that millions of insomniacs could do something useful with their time and instead of counting sheep, could practice learning a language instead. It seems that if you practice the language that you are learning at night, just before you go to sleep, you are more likely to remember it.

In this latest study, twenty participants learned in the morning and their learning was tested later the same day. An additional twenty participants learned in the evening, had a good sleep, and were then tested the following morning. Researchers discovered that sleeping between lessons led to greater long-term retention. It is also important to mention here that a number of studies indicate that learning a language can help to prevent the onset of Alzheimer's and other health conditions.

As well as practicing a language before you sleep, it is important to make language learning a daily habit. A focussed time to learn, and just before going to bed seems to be a good idea, because you are less likely to be interrupted. Learning and practicing a new language can take many forms, such as the use of subtitles in another language when watching television or listening to podcasts in Spanish.

I have always thought that in order to foster cooperation, communication and harmony, it would be a good idea if the world's three major languages: English, Spanish and Mandarin Chinese were taught in all schools, allowing effective communication across the globe and making misunderstanding and conflict less likely. Personally, I am always keen to use technology when possible, and maybe one day I will try to learn Mandarin Chinese whilst I sleep. However, this time I will be investing in a new type of pillow speaker that is connected by Bluetooth, and certainly with no more cables.

Linguaphobia

Do you suffer from 'Linguaphobia'? If you are an expat reading this, I suspect not, since most expats recognise the need to make an attempt at speaking the language of their host countries. Challenging it may be, but learning a new language does not only help expats to feel part of their adopted country, but it also helps to keep the brain active and alert, and hopefully will help to keep dementia at bay.

Sadly, it seems that all is not well in foreign language learning, according to a recent study, where experts report that Britain will be further isolated from its European partners after Brexit, because of attitudes to learning foreign languages. Apparently, following the EU referendum, many British people have become even more 'linguaphobic', relying upon a false belief that everyone across the world can speak English.

Apparently, Britain has relied for too long upon the idea that English is the world's most important language. It may come as a shock to many, but only 6 per cent of the world's population are native English speakers, with around 75 per cent of the world population unable to speak any English at all. Interestingly, 75 per cent of UK residents can only speak English, which probably explains quite a lot about issues surrounding community integration.

Over the years, I have become increasingly aware of British schools significantly reducing the amount of language teaching on their timetables. The situation has worsened in recent years, particularly since the financial crisis, and has never returned to pre-crisis levels. Britain has long been behind other European countries when it comes to language learning.

In 2004, the British Government made the decision for language teaching to become optional once students reached the age of fourteen. This led to a reduction of GCSE courses, dropping from 80 per cent to around 50 per cent of their previous levels. This, in turn, had a negative impact upon language teachers employed by schools, as well as students studying modern foreign languages at university dropping by nearly 60 per cent over the last ten years. Conversely, it is interesting to note that around 94 per cent of students in Europe are learning English, with more than 50 per cent studying two or more foreign languages.

I have often maintained that the ability to speak English, Spanish and Mandarin Chinese would ensure that our young people are in a good position to work and communicate throughout the world. I am beginning to think that my suggestions are far too modest, since the British Council announced in 2017 that the ability to speak Spanish, Mandarin Chinese, German, French and Arabic are now necessary requirements for the UK to work and trade effectively in a post Brexit world.

There are warnings too that following Brexit, there will be a shortfall of European citizens to assist with language translation and interpreter services, which the UK heavily relies upon, and is currently a billion-pound industry.

Even more worrying is a forthcoming survey of 700 modern language teachers in England commissioned by the British Council, which reports a negative attitude among both pupils and their parents towards learning foreign languages in school following the referendum to leave the European Union. There is a warning that the UK faces additional isolation following Brexit unless the country adopts a more positive attitude to learning foreign languages. The danger is that economic opportunities and bridge building across the world will suffer and result in a deterioration in economic benefits.

There are also concerns that Brexit has led to 'anti-foreigner' attitudes, with the view that once the UK leaves the European Union, foreign languages will no longer be needed; instead, exactly the opposite will be the case.

Whatever happens post Brexit, the ability to communicate with our European neighbours, as well as those further afield, will be essential for the UK to prosper and flourish. Let us hope that 'Linguaphobia' does not become the norm, and that the importance of learning a language is recognised by the wider community and not only by those living and working outside the UK.

Stoned!

Leaving messages in public places seems a strange thing to do, but I guess it has been going on for generations. You have only to look closely at ancient trees, park benches and public monuments to see those immortal words "John loves Jane", or similar words, announcing to the world undying affection of a first love, latest love or indeed any other pertinent message. I guess it is rather like the Stone Age equivalent of Facebook and Twitter, when personal (and often irrelevant) messages are declared to the world, when maybe they would be better kept to one's self.

Speaking of messages, the good people on the island of Fuerteventura are getting a little annoyed with tourists who are following the latest craze of leaving messages with stones on beaches, and building small towers with stones.

The current problem is that tourists are no longer content to wander along the beautiful white, sandy beaches of Fuerteventura, but wish to leave their mark to those who follow. I guess you could call it the human equivalent of a dog 'peeing on a lamppost'.

These tourists who visit Fuerteventura carry out message or imaginative construction activities using stones to ensure that their presence does not go unnoticed, but which local experts describe as causing a destructive impact upon the ecosystem of these beautiful beaches.

One such area, Playa de Esquinzo in Fuerteventura, is just one example that was recently highlighted where the Tourist Board wants to raise awareness that their messaging and construction activities on beaches and coastal areas are destroying and damaging the landscape. Tourists on other Canary Islands are also adopting these stone message activities without considering how their actions affect delicately balanced ecosystems. It seems that this modern-day equivalent of 'peeing on a lamppost' is not a new phenomenon. A Jewish friend recently told me that within the Jewish faith, it is customary to leave a small stone on a grave. A stone is placed by a visitor on the grave, but using only the left hand (don't ask me why).

The act of placing a stone on the grave serves as a sign to others that someone has visited the grave, and enables visitors to commemorate the burial and life of the deceased. In this way, stones are used as an act of remembrance and a lasting reminder of the deceased's life. Other historical accounts suggest that the tradition goes back to Biblical times when graves were simply marked with small stone mounds, because gravestones had not been invented. The mounds of stones helped to mark the location of the grave so that it could be found again in the future.

In addition to finding stone messages or small towers, beach walkers in the UK and US may come across a smooth pebble painted with a colourful picture of an animal or cartoon character, or simply a meaningful message. Pebble painting is yet another craze that appears to have originated in the United States and is beginning to find its way into Europe.

Amateur artists take part in painting pebbles and leaving them in public places for others to find. Brightly painted pebbles with messages and colourful patterns may be found nestling in sand dunes, on top of walls and gate posts. Some parents regard it as a welcome pastime for their children, and encourage them to take a break from their smartphones and tablets, and collect stones and decorate them. Stone painting has become quite popular in some of the UK's coastal resorts, and especially on beaches with plenty of smooth stones.

Sadly, council chiefs in the UK are not too happy with this idea, and often with good reason, as they say they pose a danger to elderly people who risk tripping over them and they are used by vandals to throw at ducks and scrawl the paint onto local war memorials. Parents are urged to be responsible and to show their children common sense when hiding these rocks, so that they don't become problems for other people and the environment.

Meanwhile, back in the Canary Islands, tourism chiefs are hoping that tourists will continue to use and enjoy its beautiful beaches, but not to feel the urge to 'dog mark' by building stone towers or painting smooth stones for others to find. Indeed, this whole issue has left tourism chiefs in Fuerteventura with stony faces, so be warned.

Food, Wine and Shopping

Chick Peas or Coco Pops for Breakfast?

I have rarely given chickpeas much thought. I know that I like them and, as vegetarians, we have regularly used them in our meals for many years. They are versatile, absorb flavours in the most delicious way and the bottled variety can usually be found at a very good price in local supermarkets.

I was interested to see that the thorny issue of chickpeas has featured quite heavily in the press recently. A Tweet by a Spanish food blogger featured a picture of her son, alongside the claim that her son doesn't know what a biscuit is, which led to an interesting spat. Apparently, the boy starts his day with a bowl of chickpeas rather than coco pops for breakfast, which brought forth a flurry of debate, and some abuse from fans of coco pops, who consider that all children should start the day with this sugary feast, washed down with chocolate milk, rather than a highly nutritious bowl of chickpeas.

Although, nutritionally, I tend to be on the side of chickpea fans, I am not sure that they are particularly good for breakfast, but then again, I have never eaten them for breakfast and intend to stick to my morning bowl of Alpen (without added sugar, of course).

The blogger raises some good points about nutrition, since it appears that breakfast for many Spanish children, as well as for children in the UK, has turned into a morning frenzy with many children being stuffed with sugar before being sent to school. Of course, in worst case scenarios, children are being sent to school without any breakfast at all, which has led an increasing demand for breakfast clubs to be established in schools in an attempt that children start the day with at least a reasonable breakfast.

What's the name for a battered chick pea? Hummus, of course, which is apparently in serious trouble due to a worldwide shortage of chickpeas. Maybe Spanish children are eating them all for breakfast? No, the real reason is that the crop has been very poor in the last few years and this has led to an inability to meet demand, which in turn has led to a price increase. The increasing demand for hummus, which is made from chickpeas, is also to blame since supermarket hummus is in high demand in the UK. The price of chickpeas is the main reason for the rapid increase in the price of hummus.

The major UK supermarkets completely ran out of the product for several weeks last year, and the ready availability of hummus is still looking doubtful, which has led to serious talk of a 'National Hummus Crisis'. After all, what exactly are people supposed to put on their pita bread? Chickpeas and hummus used to be known as 'the food for poor people'. Not any more, since hummus is now seen as a trendy addition to any sandwich, wrap, pita bread, or whatever the 'in word' for a lunchtime snack is at the moment.

The humble chickpea is grown in parts of Spain and the Canary Islands, where it is a popular addition to traditional stews and soups. Known as 'garbanzo', the chickpea has been grown in the Mediterranean, Middle East and parts of Africa for more than 7000 years. The ancient Greeks tucked into them as snacks, and they are a popular addition to Spain's national dish, 'cocido', which is a stew that consists of chickpeas and pork.

In the Canary Islands, there is a similar dish, but made with beef and chickpeas. The ingredients of these stews are not an exact one, since I guess much depends upon what the restaurant has available at the time, but I can almost guarantee that chickpeas will be lurking in there somewhere. Just don't get me started on the potential shortage of falafel!

Chocolate, Avocado Eggs and the Canary Islands

The Spanish love their chocolate. Pastries are dipped into it, biscuits are coated with it, churros are drowned in it and anything else is sprinkled with it. Chocolate is everywhere in Spain, which is not surprising, because it was the Spanish who discovered and gave birth to modern chocolate. It was Spanish explorers who brought chocolate to Europe more than 500 years ago with the addition of sugar to a bitter cocoa drink transforming it into the chocolate delight that we know today.

Indeed, it was Christopher Columbus who may be credited for being the first European explorer to encounter chocolate. It is said that Columbus intercepted a trading ship loaded with cocoa beans during one of his voyages, but thinking they were almonds he ignored the precious load.

The next step in the journey of chocolate was left to the explorer, Hernan Cortés, who may be credited for being the first European to bring chocolate to Europe. Cortés was mistaken for a God, and invited to a generous Aztec feast where he was given their prized, spicy drink of warm chocolate. Cortés was no fool, and the capitalist that he was led him to realise its value to both himself and the Spanish Crown.

The knowledge of how to turn cocoa beans into a delicious frothy drink was more a mystery that was jealously guarded by the Aztecs. It was left to Cistercian monks to get hold of and adapt the recipe that would produce chocolate for the Spanish nobility. They managed to keep their secret away from the rest of Europe for more than a century after its discovery.

Over the years, the recipe was modified to suit the European palette, which came in the form of cutting out the fiery hot peppers that the Aztecs traditionally used, replacing it with sugar cane from the Canary Islands to create the sweet chocolate that eventually became a worldwide sensation. It was decades later that a British company, founded by Joseph Fry, created the first ever chocolate bar that delivered chocolate and excess calories to the masses.

Recent shocking statistics screaming from some of the headlines this week accused Brits of eating more chocolate than anyone else in the world. Apparently, Brits munched their way through 8.4kg of chocolate each during 2017. Many commentators are suggesting that the increase in chocolate consumption is due to Brexit, with nasty rumours floating around that the price of chocolate bars will suddenly wildly increase following Brexit.

Some Brexiters are wickedly claiming that it is the fault of Remainers, who are so depressed about severing their links with the chocolate makers of Europe, that they are putting away as much as they possibly can before Brexit takes place. In response, Remainers are claiming that increased consumption is due to Brexiters who are so nervous about the implications of Brexit, that they are anxiously eating their way through the nation's chocolate bars before it is too late. It is also said that they have a longing for European chocolate, which they wish to keep secret.

Sadly, it seems that since the takeover of Cadburys by an American company, British chocolate just doesn't satisfy British taste buds any more. Some of the blame for increased chocolate consumption is also being passed onto the current trend for alcohol flavoured Easter Eggs, which apparently are going down a treat. Personally, I am not too sure about gin and tonic flavoured eggs, but I am sure that readers will tell me how wonderful they are very shortly.

Despite these interesting statistics, I was surprised to see Spain not heading towards the top of the chocoholics list. For many Spanish, there is nothing more delicious to start the day than a steaming bowl of hot chocolate in which to dip a plateful of delicious churros, which is fried choux pastry (a little like a donut that has been stretched out of all recognition). It is a highly fattening, but delicious combination, I am told.

Personally, as a vegetarian, I am very keen to get my hands on one of the new vegan avocado chocolate bars that went on sale in Europe recently. The avocado used in these chocolate bars is 100 per cent natural freeze-dried avocado, and I am reliably informed that the delicious blend of avocado and organic dark chocolate is a chocolate lover's dream. Interestingly, this product has been brought to the world by James Cadbury, who is the great, great, great grandson of Cadbury's founder. Despite this amazing news, I was very disappointed not to have received an avocado filled chocolate Easter egg this year, but I live in hope.

Just Nuts About Almonds

We know that Spring has arrived in the Canary Islands when we see the first flush of flowers on the many magnificent almond trees that embrace the islands. These beautiful flowers, which begin to open after Christmas, create a magnificent and rich landscape of colour. At the end of January and the beginning of February, almond trees demonstrate their full glory, encouraging celebrations in many towns and villages. Canarians never need much of an excuse to have a party, so this spectacle of natural beauty to celebrate the beginning of a New Year, doesn't need much encouragement.

The Canary Islands were the crossroads between Europe and the Americas for many years. As a result, the islands can boast a rich and varied cuisine, offering a unique blend of flavours that is influenced by Africa, Europe and America. Without going into too much detail here, there is accumulating genetic evidence which suggests that much of the material used for horticulture in the Americas came directly from the Canary Islands. These islands had centuries of trade with Berbers, Phoenicians, and other ethnicities in Morocco, but were only under Spanish control for about 50 years before Columbus. Many believe that the booming almond trade in the United States originates from the Canary Islands.

Many people do not give much thought to almonds, but they have always been a most important part of the cuisine of the Canary Islands. Almond products are many and varied, and used in biscuits and cakes. Almonds can also be mashed into a paste that can be spread on bread - a bit like peanut butter, but without the butter. Almond milk, almond drinks, almond wine and marzipan, as well as almond cakes can easily be found in shops and markets on the islands for most of the year.

Almond trees are found on the greener parts of the Canary Islands. In Puntagorda, on the island of La Palma, a beautiful festival is held at the end of January or beginning of February each year. Parts of Gran Canaria and Tenerife become spectacular gardens of pink and white blossom, particularly around Santiago del Teide and the slopes of Vilaflor in Tenerife.

In Gran Canaria, a visit to the Almond Flower Festival in the village of Tejeda is always a must-visit destination at this time of the year. The festival has been celebrated in this beautiful village since 1972, which acts as a reminder of the importance of almonds to the baking industry of the islands. Dancing and songs against the spectacular and colourful backdrop of the almond trees can be an unforgettable experience.

Crowds of people make their way singing and dancing to native guitar music on the narrow road leading to the church. Many dress in national costume for the event and there are opportunities to sample the local wine and almond based products. There are also opportunities to watch the almonds being cracked and maybe hear almond pickers speaking about their trade.

Spain is the world's second largest almond producer after the United States, and with a large proportion produced in the Canary Islands. It is no wonder that these nuts are so highly prized, and well worth having a party to celebrate. It is also worth remembering where the nuts come from.

Red, White or Blue?

I must first confess to having a very simplistic knowledge of wine. I know what I like and what I don't like. I will not spend a lot of time and money on fancy labels, nor will I indulge in that ridiculous time-wasting drama of 'someone who knows wine' - tasting it before it is poured knowingly by the waiter. If the wine is 'off', I would send it back. As an alternative, just sniff the cork; it really is that simple, and saves an awful lot of time.

What colour of wine do you prefer? I like white wine during a sunny lunchtime snack and maybe a chilled red during a warm evening. I tend to opt for a Canarian or Spanish wine, mainly out of loyalty to my adopted country, but I guess that my favourites are the island wines, and particularly those from Lanzarote. Now what about a blue wine?

I had the pleasure of trying a blue wine recently. I was initially a little doubtful, but since blue is my favourite colour and it was glowing temptingly in the sunshine, I didn't hesitate. After the first tentative sip, I knew that I was hooked. Not only did the deep, rich blue colour look amazing, but it suited my palette perfectly. Yes, it was on the sweet side, but it was the kind of sweetness that fits so well on a hot sunny day by the swimming pool or in a bar overlooking the sea.

To many 'wine connoisseurs', the very idea of a blue wine is truly a horrific concept, yet it is already made in several Spanish wineries. I am told that blue wine is a mix of mainly white and a little red wine, as well as freshly crushed grape juice. The blue colour is based upon using two pigments, anthocyanin, which is found in the skin of red grapes, and indigo carmine. It is best described as a blend of technology and the best that nature can provide.

I am also told that blue wine has received mixed reviews, including from the Paris 'Ritz', who described it as "surprising". Whether that is 'surprisingly good' or 'surprisingly bad', I have yet to find out, whilst the UK's Telegraph referred to it as "a gimmick", which probably means it is very nice, but they don't want anyone else to know about it.

Sadly, in Europe the new blue wine has to be labelled as an "alcoholic drink", since the authorities have decreed that it cannot be a wine, because it is blue, which leaves me very confused about the status of rosé wine.

Enterprising Spanish wineries are now producing a wide range of alternatives to the usual red and white wines. It is now possible to buy a blue, sparkling cava, a red wine that is infused with Earl Grey tea, as well as a white wine that includes a hint of Sencha tea from Japan, which sound challenging. There is also another newcomer to the range that is red and spicy, called 'Bastarde'. I am not at all sure about that one, so think I will maintain my loyalty to wines from Lanzarote and the other islands, but I do recommend that you try the blue wine if you get the opportunity.

Up the Amazon

Have you noticed how social media and the UK press love to take a swipe at Amazon whenever they can? Of course, this is just one of the least attractive parts of the human psyche; pure delight in building up and praising a sportsman, singer, film star or company, and then taking considerable pleasure in destroying them.

Personally, I have few quarrels with Amazon, since as a Brit living in Spain and the Canary Islands, I have benefited greatly from some of their services. As an author, many people buy my books from Amazon and it would be foolish to bite the hand that feeds me.

In my opinion, their Kindle books are second to none, and I doubt I would enjoy life quite so much without it. I can enjoy newly published books at a fair price whenever I wish without the delays and costs involved in ordering a physical book from the UK. No, I do not crave or wax lyrical over "the smell and feel" of a physical book; just give me my Kindle.

I am also well aware of the supposed poor working conditions in Amazon warehouses, but I suspect that conditions there are little worse than conditions faced by most unskilled workers involved in warehouse activities each day of their working lives. Indeed, I have the benefit of knowing several people who work in an Amazon warehouse who tell me a very different story to that portrayed in the press, TV and social media, so I am prepared to keep an open mind on these issues, whilst also recognising that working conditions in warehouses generally need to be improved.

I have received a few messages recently from expats complaining about some aspects of service received from Amazon in Spain. Readers may or may not know that expats living in Spain and the Canary Islands can use Amazon in a number of countries for their purchases, including Amazon UK, Amazon Germany and, one would think logically, Amazon Spain. Sadly, Amazon Spain appears to be in a state of perpetual confusion and suffering from particularly poor management when it comes to customer service in the Canary Islands, and the Spanish enclaves of Ceuta and Melilla, where services and choices offered by companies such as Amazon are of great help.

For myself, living in the Canary Islands, Amazon Spain is often a huge problem. Although I buy into Amazon Prime in Spain, which in theory, means no postage costs for most items, I invariably find that most items that I wish to order cannot be delivered to the Canary Islands anyway and, if they are, they are subject to a 'handling charge' from Correos, UPS and others acting for the Aduana (the tax authority). I rarely have any problems with Amazon UK or Amazon Germany.

Of course, it is the tax differentials between Spain and the Canary Islands that are the basis of this problem, but I am a firm believer in 'Where there's a will, there's a way'. Some time ago, anything ordered from the Spanish Peninsular would attract IGIC (the equivalent of VAT/IVA in the Canary Islands). Even though this tax is 7 per cent, there would invariably be a 'service charge' added by the courier - UPS, DHL or Correos, which would often exceed the value of the goods being delivered. The Canarian Government rightly intervened some time ago and it was then deemed that tax would only apply to items over the value of 150 euros imported into the Canary Islands.

Problem solved? Not a bit of it. Now residents of the islands find that whilst low value items do not attract tax, they still attract a 'handling charge' (DUA), which often exceeds the value of the item ordered. Whist this may be worthwhile for higher value items under 150 euros, it still means that residents of the Canary Islands, Ceuta and Melilla are not regarded as part of Spain and discriminated against. I understand that this contravenes various articles agreed by the European Union, so it rightly remains a matter of concern for many islanders.

If you do order from Amazon Spain, and find that the tax or handling charge imposed is unreasonable, my advice is that you simply refuse delivery and ask for it to be returned to the sender and purchase costs refunded. In addition, do send a complaint to Amazon so that they are fully aware of a continuing problem, although I suspect that the usual bland, 'comment bank' response will be generated. I now do this as a matter of course.

Indeed, the postman arrived a few minutes ago with a delivery of washing pods, which Amazon Spain keep urging me to try at a very special price. I paid 9.48 euros for these, but the postman has just requested 13.42 euros before he would hand them over. I refused delivery and will now buy locally. I am hoping that, in time, someone at Amazon will finally get the message and begin to treat the Canary Islands, Ceuta and Melilla as intrinsic parts of Spain.

Dog Gate

Regular readers of 'Letters from the Canary Islands' will know that I have a love-hate relationship with Amazon. Although we have 'Prime' membership with Amazon Spain, I often wonder why I bother, since most of the products that I try to order, end up with the depressing notification "This product cannot be sent to the Canary Islands, Ceuta and Melilla", which can be very irritating.

I have complained many times over the years, and pointed out that the Canary Islands are very much part of Spain, albeit with different tax regimes, and Amazon's inability to supply us in the same manner as Peninsular Spain smacks of discrimination. Sadly, Amazon rarely bother to reply, but I always feel better for firing off yet another email. This week, we had yet another 'Amazon incident'.

Our dog, Bella, is now an elderly lady of fourteen. She is totally deaf and partially blind, yet can usually reach the top of the stairs of our house before we can. Despite sleeping a lot nowadays, she has amazing bursts of puppy-like energy. Therein lies the problem, because in one of these frenetic bursts, Bella pulled a muscle in a front leg. Concerned to see her hopping around on three legs, we took her to see her vet who gave her a magic injection and tablets.

During the consultation, the vet not so tactfully mentioned that Bella was overweight; indeed, he uttered the dreaded word: "fat". Sadly, until Bella's weight is reduced, she will no longer enjoy her occasional favourite treat of a little pizza and a few chips. We were also advised not to let her run up and down stairs, since this may cause further problems for her legs.

Bella has access to everywhere in our home, so it was necessary to find something to block her access to the stairs unless we carry her up and down. I immediately thought of a 'baby gate' that parents use to stop toddlers going up and down dangerous stairs. I thought this would be easy to find, but a search of local shops, hypermarkets, baby shops, as well as second-hand shops brought only a blank look and a shake of the head.

The answer was clear, I would have to order the baby gate from Amazon even though I knew that it would be pointless to even attempt to order a baby gate from Amazon Spain, who seem to be the most chaotic of the Amazon stores that I deal with. I often find that I can order the same item from Amazon Germany or Amazon UK without a problem; totally illogical, I know. If all else fails, Amazon International will usually come to the rescue, despite additional postage costs. Sadly, this time, attempts with all Amazon stores failed, and the answer was the same; they would not delivery to the Canary Islands.

In despair, I looked at Amazon Spain and even though, as I had predicted, they would not deliver any of their range of baby gates to the Canary Islands, I found one 'third party seller' that would. It looked ideal; a baby gate that seemed as if it would work perfectly for Bella. I decided to order one; it was not available on Prime, and would cost an additional 6,99 euros for delivery. Fair enough, I thought; the order was accepted and my card debited.

Two days later, I received a very brusque email from the supplier telling me that they had cancelled the order, because they could not deliver to the Canary Islands. Apparently, the cost of postage exceeded the 6,99 euros postage that they had requested, and the true cost of postage exceeded the value of the product. They were not willing to supply the baby gate.

My response was swift and to the point. I had ordered the item in good faith from their advertisement on the Amazon website, and had agreed to pay their postage charges. They had already debited my credit card, and in doing so had completed a contract of sale. Would they agree to send the baby gate if I agreed to pay an additional charge to cover postage costs? In response, I received a very helpful reply from the company, apologising for their earlier message, and confirming that they would dispatch the baby gate on their originally advertised terms and postage costs. It seems that it does pay to complain, and I look forward to receiving Bella's 'baby gate' in due course.

The wider issue remains the same, of course, and that is the availability of products from companies such as Amazon should be similar across all the country. Yes, we live on an island, and an additional charge for postage is not unreasonable, but to be denied the range of products that are available on the Peninsular, simply because we live on an island or in one of Spain's enclaves, is both unfair, and discriminatory.

Indeed, for islanders, our choices are often limited and it is companies, such as Amazon, that could make a huge difference.

The 'B' Word

The Canary Islander

Brexit and the Faint-Hearted Expat

Of course, the tabloids never miss an opportunity to try and raise the blood pressure, so it was with some amusement that I read the headline in one tabloid this week that "Brit Expats flock from Spain because of Brexit". Seriously? I have yet to meet an established expat living in Spain, either in person or online, who is planning to return to the UK simply because of Brexit. However, I do know many who have been widowed, have significant health issues or whose businesses or relationships have collapsed and are reluctantly being forced to return to the UK, but not simply because of Brexit.

Conversely, I know of several Brits who are so upset with Brexit, high cost of living, as well as the appalling weather, that they are ready to move to Spain and other European countries at the earliest opportunity. Let's have a look at the assertion that Brits are leaving Spain by the plane load and put these headlines into some form of context.

It is true that the fall in the pound against the euro has been substantial and has had a significant impact upon the lifestyle of many British expats who are surviving on a state pension. Compared with the heady days some years ago when one pound could buy somewhere between 1.40 and 1.50 euros, there has been a considerable change in the fortunes of many expats.

It was clear to many that the pound was grossly overvalued at that time and would not last. There is also an assertion that Spain has become "incredibly expensive". Again, just have a chat with a newly arrived expat, who will leave you in no doubt as to which is the most expensive country to live in - just start off with heating bills and the price of a decent cup of coffee…

There is an assertion that the number of expats leaving Spain outnumber those now arriving in the country. I suggest that this is a highly questionable statistic and should be challenged; as with all statistics, they can be manipulated in any direction to make a good story. My own, admittedly limited contacts with removals companies, lawyers and other professionals, particularly in the Costa Blanca and Costa del Sol, tell me that the balance between those expats arriving as well as leaving broadly evens out, and that there is no expat panic. The flood of expats returning to the UK appears to be merely a convenient tabloid illusion.

There is also a huge disparity in official numbers of those living in Spain, and there could be two main factors at play here. There has been a change in municipal enrolment rules with tens of thousands of Brits previously registered, but who have returned to the UK or died, and inconsiderately forgetting to notify the town hall. Town halls benefit from having more residents, which means greater levels of funding and so there was previously no incentive for town halls to encourage people to deregister when they left the country.

A change in the law in 2010 has since meant that municipalities must now confirm if a person is still in the area every two years, or every five years if the person is listed in the Central Registry of Foreigners, which has led to many being removed from the official registers. This disparity in official numbers might also be explained by the number of foreign residents who live in Spain, but have not applied for residency.

It is uncertain issues, such as health and social care, that currently concern most British expats living in Spain, despite vague assurances from both Spanish and British Governments that all will be well. Many expats consider it unwise to move from a country where the health service is generally accepted to be under less pressure than the UK's health service at a time in their lives when they may need it.

There is also the cost of renting or purchasing a home in the UK to consider, with many expats simply no longer having significant financial resources to draw upon. It is also worth remembering that many Brits moved to Spain when they were over 65 at the beginning of 2000. Many are now left widowed, resulting in an increasing desire to return to their families in the UK. Once again, this has very little to do with Brexit. Now, let's have a look at the next tabloid scare story…

The Journey of Life

It has often been said that travel broadens the mind, which is one of the many reasons why young people particularly are encouraged to travel. I still remember, in vivid detail, the journey that I took to Germany as an insecure and impressionable thirteen-year-old. This is one incident from my childhood that I value greatly, and I will always be grateful to my parents for having the wisdom to encourage and to allow me to participate in what was at that time a new and experimental project designed to encourage post-war unity and understanding.

The journey that I experienced was part of a school twinning project, with myself and others from my school living individually with a German family, which we had no prior contact, for two weeks. One year later, the visit was reciprocated in the UK with our newly acquired German friends staying with us. For myself and many others, the visit was a huge success, and the friendship that I developed with the German boy, whose home I shared during those two weeks, was one that I greatly valued and continue to this day through emails and occasional visits.

I still recall an unpleasant night-time ferry journey from Harwich, a train journey through the Netherlands, fierce Dutch and German security police checking passports and tickets, and a combination of languages, before we finally embarked in a new and strange country that was to be my home for the next two weeks.

Nowadays, this kind of journey seems mild and quite ordinary, but at that time, the entry into post-war Europe was akin to entering an alien and potentially dangerous world. This early experience fed and nurtured my interest in countries, people and languages outside the United Kingdom, and eventually encouraged me to make a new life in another European country. It taught me much about people from outside the narrow confines of my daily life and routines in a Lincolnshire village, and nurtured my understanding of what it is to be truly European, and not simply British or English.

How times have changed, with children visiting Spain, France and Italy, and often whilst babes in arms. Overseas travel has become both easily available and affordable for many people. However, not all are able to benefit from this new freedom. Although many young people have plenty of time on their hands during the long summer holidays, they often lack the financial resources to do anything particularly worthwhile, and most do not have the funds to undertake travel that could enrich and broaden their minds.

Despite the low cost and ease of accessing other countries by using one of the cheap airlines, often the best way to see Europe is to travel by train. This is the reasoning behind an important European Union scheme for young people that is frequently ignored in the UK, which is a free Inter-Rail Pass to allow teenagers a full month of free travel around Europe.

The European Commission has set aside 12 million euros for between 20,000 to 30,000 teenagers from all over Europe to collect a free rail pass for use during the long summer holidays. The pass will allow students from the present 28 member states to ride on trains, buses, trams and ferries to visit any corner of Europe that they wish, and all free of charge.

The idea behind the initiative is to encourage young people from all backgrounds to connect with other Europeans to develop a European identity. What better way to see the sights whilst travelling relatively slowly, and absorbing the cultural idiosyncrasies of a variety of nations. Chatting to other people and sharing experiences whilst they travel will often create friendships and memories that could last for a lifetime.

I suspect that this early induction will lead to a lifelong addiction to rail travel, which is something that I doubt low cost air travel will ever achieve. Travel is a rite of passage into the world and I sincerely hope that, despite Brexit, government-funded European travel projects will continue in some shape or form. This is life education at its finest.

Eleven Women and One Astronaut

No, it is not the latest hot, porn movie or a march for equality, but the rather impressive line-up of cabinet members announced by the new Spanish Prime Minister, Pedro Sanchez. Politics aside, it is a cabinet composition that has stretched the imaginations of Spanish media headline writers, as well as briefly silencing opposition parties for just long enough for them to get their breath back following an exceptionally long and exhausting week in Spanish politics. It was a week when Spanish politics was turned upon its confused head. At the time of writing, apart from astonishment, criticism of the new line up has been unusually muted. No doubt the usual vitriol from both sides will flow again shortly.

It is not unusual for expats to lose interest or distance themselves from the politics of their home country when starting a new life in a country of their choice. That is, until the European Union referendum sparked the debate for British expats. Expats who had stubbornly refused to have anything to do with British politics suddenly became unwillingly entrenched in the debate, and often having to explain what was going on in the UK to mystified Spanish, German and Scandinavian neighbours and friends. "Were the Brits crazy?" many asked.

Suddenly, expats began to wonder about their sanity, and worry about their pensions, health entitlement, as well as family and friends who are still living in the UK. Those who had previously ignored their right to vote under the fifteen-year rule suddenly became motivated with a demand that votes for expats should be for life. After all, didn't they always have a stake in their home country?

It is under this backdrop of divisive events in the UK that many expats also became interested in political events in Spain. For many expats, an interest in the politics of their host country is a healthy one even though they cannot vote in national elections, being mostly restricted to voting in local and European elections. 'Know your neighbour' is a well-known adage, and where better to start than the politics of a country?

The new Spanish cabinet has been described by some commentators as "feminist, progressive, pro-European, pro-economy and pro-business"; it is one that prefers logic and reason over religion and belief. Accordingly, there were no crosses or bibles at the swearing-in ceremonies with the Catholic church kept at a polite and dignified arm's length, at least for the moment. It is also the first cabinet in Europe that has a female-majority, as well as one that includes an astronaut, an aeronautical engineer, a doctor, teachers, two judges, a public prosecutor and economists. Even a new Ministry has been established; the Ecological Transition Ministry, which has been formed to deal with some of Spain's (and the world's) most pressing environmental problems, particularly related to climate change.

It is now widely thought that the new Prime Minister means to govern, as well as to prepare for early elections. As well as appointing 11 capable, experienced women to his cabinet, including the Deputy Prime Minister, who is also Equality

Minister. Another woman, Teresa Ribera, is Spain's new Ecological Transition Minister who will be expected to lead the debate on climate change. Interestingly, the Prime Minister has appointed a non-separatist Catalan as Spain's new Foreign Secretary; an imaginative move that would have been unthinkable a few weeks ago.

In response to the Catalan crisis, the new Spanish Government has already lifted financial controls on Catalonia and the new government has pledged to "try to move forward" with the constitutional situation that has so far blighted attempts of reconciliation. In the end, all parties will have to talk, and so the sooner that these talks begin, the better.

I recall the words of a professor of politics who made the statement that there should be no political parties or political party whips within a legitimate democratic process, in favour of a parliament of independents voting with only with their conscience. When challenged that nothing would get done, his response was just one word: "precisely".

The silence and implied goodwill from normally vociferous observers that followed the fall of the previous government last week is probably no more than a brief pause for breath. Still, for expats, it does make a very pleasant change from listening to all those endless and argumentative Brexit debates that seem to go nowhere.

There's No Such Thing as a Free Lunch

I winced when I read an account of a recent Garden Party hosted by the British Ambassador to Spain at his residence in Madrid in honour of the Queen's birthday. The party was sponsored by a health insurer, an oil company, several banks, an accountancy firm and a communications company to name just a few. Products consumed at the party were supplied by a maker of pink gin, an ice cream manufacturer, a health insurer, an oil company, a restaurant chain, a producer of tonic water, fish from a Northern Ireland cooperative, a meat processor and a brewery. It made me wonder if the British Government (the taxpayer) had actually paid for anything; some will say that this is the point.

We are told that times are hard and the effects of the recession are still with us, but have you noticed that there always seems to be enough money around for those prestige projects? Then, of course, there is that "Brexit dividend" that we all keep hearing about; surely that would have easily have paid for a glass of cava and a cucumber sandwich without going 'cap in hand' to a range of British and Spanish businesses? Yes, I am fully aware of the argument that such events "showcase British drive and ingenuity" at a time when the UK needs to demonstrate to the world that, despite Brexit, it is still open for business, but is this really the way to do it?

I am concerned about the growing sponsorship deals by commercial companies intruding into what should be the business of the state. Surely, we all know that there is no such thing as a free lunch. Everything comes with a price tag and purpose, albeit often hidden. By accepting sponsorship of such events there is an assumption that the products and services provided by a company are endorsed and recommended by government and its agencies at the expense of others, which should not be the case.

Many years ago, I worked briefly as a civil servant, and it was always made very clear that any interaction between the government and the commercial sector should be at arm's length to avoid being seen as bias in favour of one company at the expense of another. Over the years, we have seen considerable erosion of such lofty principles, with blurring and, indeed, merging of commercial and government business.

A few days ago, the British Consulate asked if I could help to publicise an event for expats on the island. Ostensibly, it was to be about Brexit, which I am sure would be very helpful for those expats who have not yet left the island in a bid to escape the summer heat. It was only when I checked on Facebook, that I noticed that it was to be sponsored by a currency exchange company, albeit with a free drink and tapas. I realised that, once again, such sponsorship is potentially more about promoting the commercial activities of a business, rather than unbiased information for expats. I am aware of similar events for expats sponsored by a group of financial advisors; there is probably a chain of fish and chip restaurants and an online bookies already lined up to sponsor future events.

By allowing a private company to advertise and promote an event under the auspices of the British

Consul, there is an implication that the UK Government endorses their services. The currency exchange company is probably staffed by perfectly splendid and honourable people with lofty company ideals, although I note that their exchange rates are nowhere near as advantageous as those that I currently get from two rival companies, who I guess were not asked to sponsor this event. As they say, there is no such thing as free tapas, which is probably the reason why their exchange rate is not as good as it could be.

No doubt my cynicism will be rewarded with a sharp exchange of views justifying commercial sponsorship of the event on the grounds of the shrinking size of Foreign Office coffers. Despite this, I know that I am not alone in being concerned about the blurring of commercial interests and the public good. I can only imagine what my superiors in the civil service department that I worked for would have to say about that.

I have admiration for the work of the Foreign Office, its embassies and consulates in its protection, advice and support for UK travellers, businesses and expats around the world. Much of its professionalism has been based upon impartiality, and an insistence upon being seen to do the right thing.

Might I suggest a move away from freebies provided by commercial companies and instead to continue to focus with integrity upon providing unbiased advice and support to UK citizens and businesses during this disturbing period of Brexit fudge. The implied endorsement of a particular commercial activity is not the business of government and is certainly not the business of the Foreign Office and its consular services.

Brexit Going Bananas

I often write about bananas. First and foremost, I like eating them and, secondly, we have a very large banana tree growing and fruiting in our garden, which provides endless entertainment and annoyance for our dog, Bella, who, since she is partially sighted, is obsessed with the banana tree and is convinced that a gentle breeze moving the large, luxurious leaves, is actually a dangerous enemy from which she must protect us. Bananas, and similar crops, have in the past been the lifeblood of the economy of the Canary Islands and the links that these islands have with the UK are symbolised by the creation of Canary Wharf, which was the original recipient of bananas from these islands.

I have always thought that bananas are the real reason behind Brexit. Forget the accusation that "The Brits have never really liked Europe", it is really bananas that are to blame. Do you remember all the fuss about 'bendy bananas' and the myth that was so lovingly nurtured by the right wing press that straight bananas were being insisted upon by the grandees of Europe? Of course, it was nonsense, and most of the population knew it was nonsense. Despite this, it was the banana debate and other examples that became the stuff of nonsense that finally manifested itself into a call for the referendum to take Britain out of the European Union that politicians could not avoid any longer.

Bendy bananas or not, how many children and office workers include a banana as part of their lunchtime snack? The UK supermarket chain, Tesco, has upset many of its lunchtime customers recently by significantly increasing the price it charges for individual bananas. The reason for this outrage is that Tesco are now charging for single bananas instead of its usual practice of charging by weight. This has resulted in the cost of a single banana to have doubled at its Metro and Express stores. Customers were paying around 76 pence per kilogram for their lunchtime banana, which worked out at around 10 to 15 pence depending upon the size of the fruit. The new pricing at 25 pence each is often more than double the original price.

In its defence, the supermarket giant claims that expensive leases on its stores have led to the price increase, which has led to many angry exchanges on social media, leaving Tesco quaking at its very foundations and driving all the customers to Lidl and Aldi, or so we are told.

At the time of writing, Brexit negotiations are in a mess, the Government appears to have lost the plot and the opposition parties appear to be in no position to provide a workable alternative. Of course, the problem will be resolved; they always are, in time. The problem remains of course in how much damage will be done in the interim.

How many banana skins will our leaders slip on before the deal is done? Well, there's not much that I can do about it, so I'm just off into the garden to pick a nice fresh banana for my lunch. Bananas have a lot to answer for.

A Traitor in Paradise

I visited a memorial sculpture to ten sincere and brave men this week. These were ten Canarian men who were tortured and put to death for their beliefs during the Spanish Civil War. These ten men defied Franco's fascist government and were put to death by being tied in sacks filled with heavy rocks and tossed alive into the Atlantic Ocean. Almost 80 years have passed since those dark days, but now, at the point where they were deliberately drowned, a sculpture has been placed, so that the memory of these ten men and the atrocities that took place during the Spanish Civil War are not lost. Their crime was treason against the state.

In Gran Canaria's capital city, Las Palmas, excavations are currently taking place to exhume the bodies from mass graves of those killed by the Franco regime during the Spanish Civil War. The repression of civilian opponents by the Franco Regime was cruel for any person or institution thought to challenge the Republic, with any workers' movement or any political party described as being on the left of politics committing a treasonable offence.

Eighty years on, it is hoped that exhumation of bodies from a mass grave will begin to repair the nightmares suffered by families and friends of those buried, and paid with their lives for the repression imposed by the Franco regime. Memories of the Civil War continue to be powerful reminders of the evils of a fascist dictator that ignored the rules of basic humanity.

I was suddenly reminded of Spain's horrific and bloodthirsty past perpetrated on these beautiful islands this week when I read a proposal from a Conservative councillor in the UK stating that opposing Brexit should be made an act of treason, and publishable by life in prison. To further strengthen the argument for 'treason', a statement from a UK Brexiteer, David Bannerman, a Conservative Member of the European Parliament, suggested that the revision of the 1351 Treason Act should also apply to EU loyalists; those who undermine the UK through "extreme EU loyalty".

As far as I am aware, in law, treason is a crime that covers some of the more extreme acts against one's country or monarch. History gives us many examples of treason, including Judas Iscariot who betrayed Jesus, and Henry VIII who had two of his six wives executed for alleged adultery on the grounds that such infidelity was 'treason'. The current US President, Donald Trump, is accused of 'treason' because of his alleged links with Russia. Other examples of so-called 'treason' are often little more than action by dissidents, which may happen to upset or offend others who are, or wish to be, in power.

One thing is clear, the definition of 'traitor' needs extreme care in its application. To describe those who disagree or are opposed to the foolishness of Brexit as 'treacherous' is inaccurate and does no credit to those who imply treason. There are many British citizens living and working in Europe, as well as many Europeans living and working in the UK, who are passionate about wanting the UK to remain in the European Union; they are vocal about it and support and donate to causes that are attempting to promote an alternative point of view. This does not make them traitors; indeed, one could make an argument to the contrary.

History is supposed to help us to avoid the mistakes of the past. If we look at the history of Spain's Civil War, and how it divided and ruined a prosperous country, together with the hurt that continues to this day, we all need to be more careful about the language that is used to challenge opponents.

Needless to say, many were surprised to hear Bannerman's proposals, with some asking what he would suggest as an appropriate punishment to be applied to "extreme" EU loyalists, currently known as 'Remainers'. It should be remembered that 63 per cent of the UK population did not vote for the nonsense that is Brexit; we are still allowed to hold alternative views to those expressed by Bannerman, Rees-Mogg, Gove, Johnson and others. We are still allowed to protest, demonstrate and articulate views that may be contrary to the views of the Brexiteers; it is not treachery. Fortunately, the new proposals do not call for the death penalty to be applied, but encourages prison sentences for those found guilty. Well, that's all right then; I rather like the idea of a few months free accommodation in the Tower of London.

Getting Used to the Unexpected

The Virtual Spanish Hotel

Our first holiday in Spain some years ago was not a great success. We had booked into a major tour company's "flagship hotel", as it was described, only to find a bed containing the residue of its previous occupant, a couple of cockroaches and the distressing remains of a previous night's curry in the toilet. Needless to say, we complained and were moved to another room. It was not the best introduction to our first holiday in Spain.

What do you look for in hotel or self-catering accommodation? I have always maintained that if I am going to spend hard-earned cash on holiday, I require the standard to be at least the same, if not better than our accommodation at home. Like many visitors, I dislike those narrow, uncomfortable, wooden beds and thin mattresses that are so popular in most Spanish and Canary Islands' budget hotels and bungalow complexes. Insufficient hot water, no kettle, and ineffective air conditioning are all areas that are likely to generate a negative review on Trip Advisor.

Nowadays, my demands also include free Wi-Fi, and not just a pathetic signal in reception, but one that I can actually use in the hotel bedroom, without an additional charge. I have this at home, so why not on holiday? Sadly, even some of the four- and five-star hotels on these islands rarely offer this facility and is a source of constant complaints from guests. According to a recent tourism fair in Spain, much of this is about to change.

How about a hotel room that automatically adjusts to the needs, language and nationality of its guests, virtual reality headsets instead of brochures, as well as facial recognition instead of a key card to enter your room? Once guests' personal details and preferences are logged into the system, the room will automatically change the digital pictures in the room from Picasso to Monet, monitor the room temperature and adjust the lighting to personal requirements.

Hotels will be able to provide a facility whereby guests can order a pizza in 40 languages; why one would want to do this is open for discussion, but I guess it is a nice gesture to while away an hour or two. Room locks will also be 'intelligent' and will open and close according to the WhatsApp settings on a guest's smartphone. What about those ghastly wooden beds and thin mattresses? Well, new ones will have sensors built into the mattress, which will monitor movements and sense when the occupant awakes, and will notify staff to bring a cup of coffee and croissant to get the morning off to a good start. However, I am not sure that guests will approve of bed sensors monitoring the time, quantity and speed of their lovemaking.

Needless to say, the main benefit of these new systems is not always for the guests' benefit, but to improve "productivity". If, for instance, a large number of British guests are due to check in, additional quantities of bacon, black pudding and eggs will be ordered automatically to cope with the copious demand for those much loved 'English breakfasts'.

Virtual Reality headsets are currently being used, both in Spain and Morocco, to present hotels to tour companies instead of brochures. Travel agents can take a virtual tour of the bedrooms, pool area, restaurant and other facilities, which will give a much more realistic indication of likely customer satisfaction.

In some hotels, there will be beacons and sensors fitted in rooms that will make use of guests' smartphones to monitor at what time they visit the pool, how long they stay in their rooms and how vigorously they brush their teeth. Maybe it will also monitor how much toilet paper is used on 'curry and lager' nights and order additional quantities according to need? Complicated algorithms will be able to monitor their guests' habits in order to sell additional products and services, as well as special offers to encourage them to return to the hotel. The system will also be able to determine whether guests arrive with their usual partner and children or with someone else - in which case, if the guest does not eat in the dining room, a special meal will be sent to the hotel room, complete with a bottle of champagne.

Is all this going a little too far, do you think? Few of these new services will be able to operate without considerable intrusion into the personal data of guests, which I suspect many will be unhappy about. As much as I love gadgets and applaud some of the new technology, and particularly improved beds, I suspect that most visitors will be content with a clean room, a comfortable bed, a kettle and good quality Wi-Fi.

Bed and Breakfast, but no Roof

It is holiday time again, and the 'big getaway' is about to begin in most countries. Those of us who live in Spain and the Canary Islands will hardly be surprised to read that Spain and the USA are jointly the second most popular countries for tourists to visit in the world with 75.6 million visitors each. Figures show Spain and the USA just behind France, which had 82.6 million visitors.

With all this holiday travel, and particularly during the peak holiday season, finding sufficient accommodation for all manner of guests with different budgets can be a problem. In the Canary Islands, for instance, it used to be a simple matter of recommending a tried and trusted hotel for visiting friends, yet this is currently becoming more of a problem with most hotels at full capacity for much of the year.

Whilst innovative ideas, such as AirbnB have helped to ease the load, this form of accommodation is increasingly being eyed with suspicion, especially by tourism officials who are concerned about wide variations in the quality of such accommodation, as well as tax and local authority officials who are concerned that taxes are not being paid.

I was intrigued to hear about one innovative offering from Airbnb on the deliciously unconventional Spanish island of Ibiza. Since accommodation on the island is in short supply, and prices have increased to unrealistic levels, some locals are offering a bunk bed on their balconies for just 50 euros a night. One such 'hostel' offers up to nine bunk beds on a small balcony. Guests have use of the bathroom and living room, although understandably, this area is heavily monitored with a security camera.

If this isn't quite up to usual standards, guests can opt to stay in a wooden shack and delivery vans converted into 'caravanettes', although these alternatives are more expensive at 90 euros per night, but they do have the added advantage of a roof. It is probably worth paying extra for protection during a sudden storm or a mosquito attack. Intending guests might find it useful to know that Ibiza is an all-day party island where quality sound proofing could be quite useful, particularly at night.

One enterprising businessman in Spain recently bought an old plane from a bankrupt airline with a view to converting it into premium accommodation for tourists. I am often told how comfortable planes are to sleep in during long haul flights, so logic tells me that they could make comfortable night time accommodation on the ground too. This form of holiday accommodation could well appeal to aviation fanatics and those seeking something different. Personally, once I have arrived at my destination and left the plane, the last thing that I would want to do is to spend my holiday in one; still, it takes all sorts.

This businessman may well be on to something big, since there are a number of converted planes around the world that have been successfully converted into hotels, bars, restaurants, homes and even a McDonalds! There is one plane in Georgia that has been converted into a kindergarten, which will no doubt appeal to aspiring pilots of the younger generation. In New Zealand, one 1950s Bristol Freighter twin engine aircraft that was used in the Vietnam War has been converted into a motel, although guests have to pay extra to sleep in the cockpit. Another airplane in the Netherlands has been converted into a romantic getaway with all those holiday essentials, including a spa, jacuzzi, infrared sauna, mini bar and three flat screen televisions. I am curious to know what happens in an infrared sauna…

Personally, I think I will give these alternatives a miss, since I am desperate to stay in one of the new 'virtual reality' hotels with accommodation that adjusts to the specific needs of individual guests, such as the prototype recently demonstrated at Madrid's tourism fair, but that is a story for another time. Finally, if you find yourself sleeping in unusual holiday accommodation, such as a garage, kennel or disused swimming pool, do please let me know.

It's a Crazy, Crazy Expat August

The usual August madness has swept across Spain with a vengeance. First of all, it was 'refreshing' to see that the reliable Swedish emporium of all things good and wholesome, namely Ikea, haven't lost their sense of humour in marketing a lavatory brush given the appealing name of 'Farage'. Sadly, Ikea has since disassociated itself from the toilet brush story and claims it is 'fake news', but all is not lost since they are selling a doormat under the name of 'Boris', which is the name of a small town in Denmark. It is a great pity about the loo brush though, since I rather like the idea of turning the name 'Farage' into a verb and would quite enjoy "faraging" the loo.

Forgive me, but I am having an August moment, and I promise that I won't mention the table (strong and stable) sold under the name of Theresa... Whilst we are on the subject of Ikea, I just wish one could get a decent cup of coffee there and not a mug of lukewarm sludge that appears to have been left over from the weekend. Yes, I know it is cheap, but I really shouldn't have to strain it through my teeth...

There was the amazing and heart-warming story of the British expat living in Spain (now given the name, 'Eileen Dover') who 'fell off' a cruise ship during a spin across the Adriatic and spent ten hours in the sea.

I will dare to ask the obvious question that BBC reporters carefully omitted from their interview, but everyone really wanted to ask. Was the poor woman so tanked up with gin and tonics that she just slipped off the edge of the ship, or was she pushed? Sorry, it may seem an indelicate question, but I just need to know. In any case, despite thinking that after ten hours bobbing around in the Adriatic she would look rather like a prune, she looked in remarkably good condition and seemed to be very perky when chatting to the press.

Maybe I shouldn't suggest that she looked as if she had returned home after a really good night out with the girls, but I will. Anyway, I am delighted that she was rescued and appears to be making a good recovery from her ordeal. Clearly, she kept well away from sharks.

Some Spanish resorts are so fed up with British holidaymakers that they are posting advertisements and Twitter posts urging tourists to jump off balconies. "Balconing is Fun" the posters declare. Balconing involves jumping into a swimming pool from a hotel or apartment balcony, or climbing from one balcony to another. These sick posters and tweets mock the deaths of tourists engaging in a sport that is apparently growing in popularity amongst some mainly young and impressionable British holidaymakers. This activity often results in an unpleasant death or very serious injury, so is a very unkind way to get the message across.

One tragic incident took place this month when a 20-year-old British holidaymaker tried to "take a poo" over the edge of his balcony before plunging six floors and landing on his head. At the time of writing, the young man remains in a critical condition.

A different approach to unthinking and inebriated holidaymakers is currently being considered by the regional government of the Balearic Islands. The good people of Mallorca, Ibiza and Minorca are so fed up with the chaos that many British tourists bring to their beautiful islands, that they are proposing to ban 'all inclusive' drinks, which is a thoughtful alternative to suggesting that holidaymakers jump off their balconies. Maybe this will help to curb Brits from being over enthusiastic drinkers during their holiday? Somehow, I have my doubts that this will work, but it is a kinder alternative.

The story of the elderly British holidaymaker staying in a Benidorm hotel also hit the headlines this month. This holidaymaker did not enjoy her sea, sun and sangria, and reportedly complained that the hotel had too many Spanish holidaymakers staying there and why couldn't they holiday somewhere else? "I'm not a racist", she firmly declared. Surprisingly, the tour operator gave her a refund; personally, I would give her a map and point out that Benidorm is in Spain and not the UK. Maybe she had lost her glasses and had planned to holiday in Blackpool instead?

Ryanair also deserves a mention, since an Irish holidaymaker, frustrated following a four-and-a-half-hour delay from Spain, refused to pay for a small tub of Pringles and a bottle of water for his stressed and over tired five-year-old daughter, and was threatened with arrest when they landed. The passenger was entitled to a compensation voucher that would easily have covered the cost of the water and Pringles if he had remembered to collect it from the departure lounge, but he was more concerned about his young daughter. An announcement was made to the entire cabin that police would deal with him upon arrival. The airline rightly commented that they "do not tolerate unruly, disruptive or unlawful behaviour". Ryanair, please remember to apply this edict on my next Ryanair flight when I am surrounded by abusive and inebriated passengers.

At least EasyJet had the good sense to cancel a flight to Spain at the last minute when they decided that their Belfast crew was too tired to fly to Mallorca. Right, let us all remember that in August, if we are too tired, it is OK not to turn up for work. That goes for doctors, nurses, supermarket staff and hotel receptionists. Clearly, they are sensible people at EasyJet.

There is never a dull moment when watching the Brits at play in Spain during the month of August. Spain is the number one choice for holidays for many Brits and it is easy to see why. The carefree lifestyle, relatively cheap flights and accommodation, easy and cheap access to alcohol and drugs (if you must), beautiful beaches, endless sunshine and friendly locals all add up to a winning combination. The behaviour of Brits on holiday is often hilarious, sometimes embarrassing and occasionally very sad. Soon, August will be over and we can all get back to normal.

No Home in the Sun

The Canary Islander

Poverty in the Canary Islands

As we prepare for the Christmas festivities, maybe an article about poverty is not what many will expect, but maybe it is the most important time to discuss a subject that we are all aware of, but feel helpless to do anything about. At least in the Canary Islands, we can offer a little good news that should have a positive impact upon many people in need.

I sometimes write about both homelessness and food aid in the Canary Islands, which surprises some and annoys those who believe that I should somehow focus my time upon extolling the virtues and beauty of these wonderful islands, and act as an unofficial holiday promoter.

Since I do not work for the tourism industry or am responsible to the island government, I feel that my time is better spent opening the eyes of those who have been seduced by the island dream to what is really going on behind those glossy brochures and slick television advertisements.

Yes, these are wonderful islands to visit, live, work and play, but the unemployment situation is horrendous, particularly for young people, and the lack of affordable housing is at crisis levels, so that we have many residents who are either homeless or relying on food banks to survive.

Despite those glossy brochures and 'all you can eat and drink' hotel deals in this 'alternative island universe', this is not the reality that many people face each day of their lives.

The Canary Islands are not alone in this shame. Poorly publicised statistics show that between 2013 and 2017, around 230 homeless people died on the streets of Britain. Between 2017 and 2018, 440 people have died, which is almost twice as many in a quarter of the time. How any society can allow this to happen, and how any government can rest easy with these appalling statistics, I do not know.

The good news is that in Gran Canaria, the city of Las Palmas has recently created the first day centre for homeless people with an investment of around 700,000 euros from the Canary Islands Development Fund. This building will be accessible for all as it will have an elevator, stairs and bathrooms especially adapted for people with reduced mobility. This refurbishment project began in 2017 with the first phase of demolition of the interior.

It is hoped that this new facility will open in February 2019, and will be the first day centre for homeless people in the Canary Islands. The day centre will provide a reception area, medical and administrative offices, training rooms, a hairdressing salon, toilets, and bathrooms adapted for people with reduced mobility, as well as an outdoor area that will be used as a rest area. The first floor will provide a kitchen, a dining room with capacity for 60 people, luggage storage, restrooms and showers for residents, a locker room for staff, offices, a warehouse and a cleaning room. The third floor, which is currently under construction, will see the creation of 34 residential spaces, so that homeless people can spend the night in the new centre.

In another welcome move, the Government of the Canary Islands has received 1,787,000 euros from the European Aid Fund for the Most Disadvantaged, which is the second of three payments to the Spanish Red Cross and the Spanish Federation of Food Banks in the Canary Islands.

The European Aid Fund is jointly funded by the European Union and the Spanish Government and is intended to promote social cohesion, to reinforce inclusion and to contribute to the goal of eradicating poverty.

Food aid is given to various institutions to distribute to the population according to different categories, such as those with low incomes, mothers with new babies, unemployed people, as well as those identified as being within the poverty index.

In the Canary Islands, the money allocated to the purchase of food amounts to almost 5,300,000 euros divided into three periods throughout the year.

The 'food basket' contains about fourteen products, such as white rice, cooked beans, UHT milk, olive oil, canned tuna, pasta, tinned tomatoes, biscuits, canned green beans, canned fruit in light syrup, powdered chocolate, infant bottles of fruit and chicken, infant cereals and milk powder.

During the early days of the recession, politicians in both Spain and the UK were fond of using placatory phrases, such as "We are all in it together".

Clearly, we are not and never will be. These islands have the potential to be of enormous benefit to all its citizens, and not just the mega hotels and businesses that are often based in other countries and have very little positive impact upon the local economy.

It is with this in mind that I read with interest a recent report from the Government of the Canary Islands that the new tourism strategy for the islands between now and 2025 will contain a commitment to the whole of society, and with the aim of increasing the quality of life for all. Let us hope that this really will be the case, and not just empty words.

Living in a Hayloft or a Pod

The severe social and economic consequences of failing to provide sufficient housing for increasing populations is at last beginning to dawn upon national and local politicians in many countries. For far too long, governments of all political shades have ignored the issue of providing sufficient numbers of high quality, low cost housing for sale, as well as for rent.

It is disturbing, inhumane and unacceptable to see people living on the streets in some of the most prosperous countries in the world.

The Canary Islands and Spain are not immune from this issue, since increasing demand for both permanent, as well as holiday accommodation is a growing problem. A few interesting, as well as challenging ideas, are beginning to emerge that may help.

A company in the city of Barcelona has recently announced a plan to build an apartment that will house 15 people in tiny capsules that will cover an area of just 100 square metres. The idea for the project comes from a Japanese company called Haibu, where clients sleep in a pod that contains little more than a bed and a TV attached to the ceiling.

The word 'haibu' means beehive in Japanese, with the company commenting that people are social creatures who were meant to live in communities that help each other out, rather like bees in a hive.

These pods are intended for permanent residents of the city and not for tourists. Each pod is 120cm wide, 120cm high and 200cm long. There is a bed and a headboard that can also be used for storage, shelves, a folding table, a wall socket and a USB charger.

There are also communal areas, such as a shared bathroom and kitchen facilities. With rapidly increasing rents in the city, the company believes that its charge of 200 euros per month for each 'room' is an attractive proposition. The company believes that its pods are a better option than a hostel or sleeping on the streets, and will allow clients some privacy until their financial situation improves.

City authorities are not happy with the idea, commenting that there is no room for such a project in Barcelona, and warn that any housing unit must have a surface area of at least 40 square metres, which means that this company will never obtain the necessary operating licenses. Some commentators have already made the point that there is already a range of similar accommodation available in Spain's cemeteries, called coffins.

There are other options to consider. For instance, the Municipality of La Orotava in Tenerife has recently developed an imaginative idea that will help to ease the shortage of homes for local residents.

The plan involves the renovation of over 300 barns and haylofts across the municipality that are currently abandoned. It is thought that each hayloft could provide a home for a family of up to 10 people.

Haylofts were traditional buildings that were mostly built in the higher areas of the island. They could help to solve the problems of lack of housing, and local councillors assure residents that those who used them many years ago were kept warm in winter and cool in summer.

Canary Islanders know a thing or two about unusual housing, since many residents have lived and continue to live in traditional housing, such as caves, across several of the islands.

Over many years of disuse and neglect, many of these haylofts will require careful rebuilding and renovation, but will be a much a cheaper and faster alternative to building new, traditional homes.

This imaginative idea of converting 300 barns will not only provide homes for local people, but will ensure that these attractive traditional buildings can be preserved for historical interest in the future.

The difficulties of earning a large enough salary to be able to purchase a property in Spain has led to another dimension within the Spanish housing market, and that is through the concept of 'bare ownership', which some say is macabre, yet is perfectly legal. Elderly property owners are selling their homes for half the market value to willing buyers on condition that they can live out their final days in their home. When the elderly person dies, the new owner is then free to move in or sell the property at market value. Despite conditions attached to such a deal there appears to be no shortage of buyers tempted by the longer-term benefits of the seller's death.

In the future, we will see many new initiatives designed to ease the shortage of housing across Europe. Some ideas will make better use of existing space through good planning and thoughtful design. Other schemes will no doubt focus mainly upon the profit motive, with little thought and compassion for those who will spend their lives there. Having a home is a basic human right and failing to provide sufficient homes demonstrates a breakdown in the traditional, embedded values of society.

It's Very Easy to be Conned

The lurid red leaflets advertising his range of 24-hour plumbing services in both English and Spanish have been blocking up our letter box for the last twelve years. Proudly declaring that he has been in the plumbing business for over thirty years, Juan, as I will call him, was clearly a reliable professional, or so we thought. When our toilet suddenly decided it needed some technical assistance, we decided to call him. How wrong we were!

From the moment that Juan and his equally burly henchman walked into our home, I felt uneasy about the two men. My usual well-honed character radar was already flashing warning signs due to their over excitable levels of 'easy talk', which always makes me suspicious. Recovering from a heavy cold at the time, clutching a handful of 'Kleenex' tissues and after downing the Spanish equivalent of 'Lemsip', I showed Juan to the offending toilet. I was impressed, as well as disgusted, when Juan plunged his hand inside the toilet and appeared to grope erotically around the inside of the bowl with intense satisfaction. I guess it takes all sorts in life, but I was relieved that we had poured substantial quantities of strong disinfectant into the bowl before his arrival. He could at least have worn rubber gloves, I thought.

Juan confirmed my initial diagnosis that the plunger mechanism needed replacing. He nodded wisely, but then went on to explain that the sewage outlet pipe appeared to be blocked. Nothing too serious that would need machinery to unblock the pipe, but suggested that a dose of strong acid would do the trick. I asked how much this would cost and he explained that it would be about 25 euros. I agreed, and Juan and his colleague went off into town to get a new plunger mechanism, as well as the acid.

A short time later, the pair returned, carrying a new plunger, as well as a battered plastic container, which I guess was holding about five litres of liquid. I was presented with a receipt for twelve euros for the plunger, but there was no mention of the cost of the acid. Juan proceeded to fit the new plunger and to pour the liquid down the toilet. Both he and the toilet made impressive gurgling sounds; he was after all, a very large man who I suspect had a very large, late breakfast just before his visit. I was asked to examine the outflow from the inspection chamber in the road. It all seemed to be flowing well. Juan nodded with satisfaction and I asked for the bill.

At this point Juan became very vague and started to jot down a number of incoherent figures. He finally declared that the cost of 25 litres of "very special acid" at a cost of 15 euros per litre, together with 12 euros for the new plunger and his labour charges amounted to the grand total of 550 euros. I laughed, and told him that he had made a mistake. He shook his head seriously and attempted to explain that the "special acid" was one available only to certain plumbers who had authorisation to use the stuff. The alternative would be to employ a commercial rodding service that would cost much more. I asked him to show me the receipt for the acid that he had purchased, but he declined, telling me that it was his own mix (of water, I began to suspect).

As we disputed and argued, the atmosphere grew to a level where we were getting nowhere. I resolutely refused to pay up, whilst Juan and his henchman became more threatening and intimidating. The price came down to 500 euros, 450 euros, 400 euros and eventually to 300 euros. I refused to pay until I had been given a detailed invoice and could check the prices for myself after obtaining a second opinion from a specialist. In any case, I did not have that kind of money readily available, and so the plumbing pair insisted that they drive me to the nearest cash machine to relieve me of the cash. I refused to comply and asked the pair to leave our home, which they refused.

At this point, I called the police to ask for their assistance. When overhearing my conversation with the police, Juan immediately changed his attitude and asked how much I would be prepared to pay for the job. I offered one hundred euros, which I considered to be generous, and suspect it was double the price that the job was worth. Juan accepted, declaring that he was "very angry", and the troublesome duo finally left.

A short time later, two gun-toting Policia Nacional officers arrived at our house. They were polite, friendly and very helpful. I told them the story, which they carefully listened to. They advised me that I could make a formal complaint against the plumber at the police station, as they were undoubtedly committing a crime by advertising their services without an individual or company identification number, giving no business address or full name. However, as I had invited Juan into our home, and did not ask for a quotation of price or see their identification, they had not committed a crime. Indeed, it could be argued that I had committed a crime by paying them 'black money' for the job, which would not be declared to the tax authorities. I accepted their point, and realised that I had created a series of traps for myself by not being sufficiently vigilant in checking their credentials. Usually, I would ask a trusted neighbour or friend for recommendations, but sometimes circumstances force us to stray away from our normal pattern of behaviour.

Nearly every week, I hear stories of expats in Spain and the Canary Islands being victims of fraud, yet I had completely forgotten the key principles of checking the validity of tradesmen before letting them into our home. Admittedly, I was not feeling very well at the time, but this failure could have ended up costing me a lot of money, as well as more unpleasantness. I am now pleased to report that our toilet is flushing well, although I remain flushed with embarrassment. I have learned yet another serious lesson in life.

Unemployment Good, Employment Bad

I heard a UK economist on the radio this week complaining about high employment levels in the country. Apparently, high employment is bad for the economy, since it forces wage and salary levels upwards, which is bad for UK exports and the overall economy. Conversely, high unemployment level is preferable, according to this economist, since it creates "a competitive employment background", which results in wage stability and even a reduction in production costs (for this read overall wage stagnation and depression).

Thankfully, I am not an economist, but I guess that most people will view this as simple exploitation of labour. Whether or not it is a good idea will no doubt depend upon your political and social views. Personally, I cannot think that anyone in their right mind would find unemployment acceptable under any circumstances. Still, we are told that we now live in a post-truth world where anything goes.

Unemployment is supposed to be at its lowest level in the UK for many years, even though many jobs are of fragile status by working within the 'gig economy' or zero-hours contracts. In contrast, unemployment in Spain and the Canary Islands is still at worryingly high levels. Unemployment in the Canary Islands remains stubbornly at around 31 per cent, which is one of the highest in Europe. For those under 25 years old, the unemployment rate is at a shocking 56 per cent, accompanied by severe social consequences, as well as destroying dreams and confidence for a generation of young people.

It was encouraging to hear this week that several new and imaginative schemes designed to reverse the trend are currently being deployed in the Canary Islands. The Government of Gran Canaria has recently announced that 220 unemployed people over the age of 45 years and without previous skills will be trained as skilled metal workers in the Port of La Luz in Las Palmas de Gran Canaria, which is one of the largest employers on the island. The main employer on the site, Femepa, operates 1,600 companies that have job opportunities for welders and electricians, but often faces difficulties in finding workers to fill these vacant posts.

Cars, lorries and motorcycles regularly need repairs, and in the Canary Islands there are over 4,500 elevators that need to pass a safety inspection each year.

This new project will also provide job opportunities for the refurbishment of homes and the maintenance of hotels. 220 people will be invited to participate in training courses to work in the metal sector, and Femepa and the island government hope that all those who complete the training will be offered jobs.

These courses are intended for those who have been unemployed for over a year, are over 45 years of age, immigrants, victims of gender violence or have a low level of education.

The Government of Gran Canaria has also announced that it will employ 50 unemployed people to work full time for six months in reforestation tasks.

This programme is aimed at women who are victims of gender violence, immigrants and those over the age of 45 years, so that they can learn a trade in a sector in which there is a real demand for professionals with appropriate skills. This specific group of unemployed people will soon learn how to fell trees, climb trees, provide trees with sufficient water and to use specific machinery for forestry tasks.

Both projects are relatively small scale, yet are an attempt to bring hope for the future and an escape for many people who are desperate to break away from the misery of unemployment. In this 'Alice in Wonderland' world, I wonder what the UK economist who spoke so favourably of the benefits of unemployment would think of these attempts to give people some hope for the future?

The Great Spain Pension Robbery

I recently came across many pensioners protesting in the capital city of Las Palmas de Gran Canaria. This protest was just one taking place in a hundred Spanish cities to raise the plight of pensioners in society. In the Canary Islands, hundreds of people took to the streets in La Laguna in Tenerife and Las Palmas de Gran Canaria to ask for support in their ongoing struggle to preserve the public pension system. Pensioners are protesting against the actions of the previous government, and complaining that it had raided the country's pension funds in order to bail out the Spanish banks during the financial crisis.

Most Spanish pensioners complain that their pensions do not give them enough to live on. Average pensions in Spain are around 1100 euros each month, with the general pension at around 950 euros, which seems generous when compared to UK pensions. Crude comparisons between the two countries are unreliable, since the level of unemployment in Spain continues to be very high, whereas it is very low in the UK.

As a result, many Spanish pensioners are responsible for supporting their families, as many of whom continue to live with their parents during troubled financial times. It is within this context that Spanish pensions are seen as necessary to support the wider family and not just a single person or a couple.

Incidents such as this often trigger memories from my childhood, and this encounter was no exception. My memory went back to returning home from primary school one day, and complaining bitterly to my mother about my pocket money. When compared to the amount that my friends told me they received, the amount I was given was miserly and I made my feelings very clear.

Overhearing the fuss that was going on, my elderly grandfather, who was staying with us at the time, quietly took me to one side and asked why I thought I deserved any pocket money at all. I remember giving him a list of reasons, which he carefully listened to, before telling me that he never received any pocket money. His father had died when he was very young and my grandfather had to work from a very young age in order to keep the family together.

He remembered the sheer joy and appreciation when he received his very first "Old Age Pension", as it was called at that time. The pension was five shillings each week, which for many pensioners meant the difference between basic survival or being forced to live in the workhouse. Lecture over, my grandfather patted me on the head, put his hand in his pocket and handed me some coins with his usual comment of "Don't tell your mother".

The first non-contributory British pension began in January 1909. The weekly pension was five shillings each week (25 pence) paid to all people over the age of 70, and 7 shillings and sixpence paid to married couples. Five shillings (25p) is about £20 in today's value, but measured by the increase in average earnings it is more like £112, which is less than the current basic state pension of around £130.00 weekly.

UK Pensions were kept deliberately low in order to encourage people to make their own provision for old age. In order to be eligible, the applicant had to be of "good character", earn less than 31 pounds ten shillings a year and have been a UK resident for at least 20 years. There were other conditions too, such as not being convicted of drunkenness, not held in prison or a 'lunatic asylum' or habitually out of work; they were harsh times.

Back to the protests in Spain, which were intended to remind everyone that the pensioners' demands are everyone's business. These protestors are highlighting the problems faced by pensioners in Spain, such as loss of purchasing power that leaves them feeling helpless. They were also asking for the repeal of reforms in the labour market, which they claim has led to unstable employment opportunities for young people. Government proposals to promote private pension funds are described as privatisation of the public pension system 'by the back door'.

Looking after the well-being of older people is one of the elements that constitutes a civilised society. Although these issues are within different cultural contexts, the struggles by pensioners in both Spain and the UK have a similar resonance, which is fairness and a desire to be heard.

Fuel Poverty

We paid our electricity bill this week, or rather it was debited from our bank account without any warning. It has always irritated me that the electricity companies in Spain and the Canary Islands feel that they can take whatever they wish from our bank account without letting us know in advance; it is the same with the water company too. In the Canary Islands, electricity and water bills usually arrive two or three weeks after the payment has been taken from bank accounts, which makes careful budgeting, particularly for those on a low income, very difficult.

I am sure that most people find that monthly electricity bills increase and rarely is there any movement downwards. In our home, over the last few years, we have gradually changed to energy efficient lighting and appliances, but the increase in cost whilst consumption remains steady is often staggering.

It is of course, the poorest in society that are most affected by high electricity bills. Terms such as 'Fuel Poverty' or 'Energy Poverty' are some of the current meaningless phrases designed to make this serious issue somehow socially more acceptable. For many people, this can mean an impossible choice between keeping warm or eating. In the Canary Islands, those regarded as 'vulnerable', as well as large families can apply for a 'social bonus', which is designed to ease the cost of such bills by providing a discount. Unfortunately, as is the case with many such schemes in Spain, the system is unnecessarily complicated and bureaucratic, which many families simply do not understand and such schemes often end up causing more harm than good.

The best way of avoiding energy poverty is to reduce the cost of electricity through the promotion and investment in renewable energy. This will come in time, assuming that the oil companies and politicians allow it, but in the meantime, efforts are being made to encourage municipalities to provide emergency fuel aid for those families that cannot pay their electricity bills and the supply is cut off. Local politicians are rightly making the point that that residents of the Canary Islands have a right to receive electricity at a price that is equivalent to residents living in Peninsular Spain, even though the costs of producing electricity on the islands are three times as high.

In the Canary Islands, we have an abundance of sunshine, wind and wave power, but the dilatory manner in which these renewable sources are being utilised is staggering. There are examples to the contrary, of course, with the island of El Hierro leading the way with massive investment in renewable sources, which is already making a huge difference to the lives of islanders, as well as a massive reduction in carbon emissions and is often quoted as a positive example by researchers in other countries.

The Canary Islands are located just a short distance from Africa, and it was interesting to hear researchers recently claim that the installation of huge numbers of solar panels and wind turbines in the Sahara Desert would have a major impact on rainfall, vegetation and temperatures. The action of wind turbines and solar panels would double the amount of rain that currently falls on the Sahara, which would have a huge and positive impact upon the region, allowing vegetation to flourish.

In addition, according to the researchers' calculations, a massive installation of solar panels and wind farms in the desert would generate more than four times the amount of energy that the world currently uses each year. If such plans were ever to come to fruition, it could potentially end the issue of fuel poverty once and for all. However, one can only imagine the blocking mechanisms of the oil industry and investors in the energy market.

Use It or Lose It!

It was really good to read in the news this week that the Canary Island of Fuerteventura will once again provide a Beach Library at the beach of Los Pozos. It is a simple concept, users can read books and magazines, as well as participating in a range of activities, such as sports and workshops connected to reading. This library will include books in various languages, and readers can even take their book home with them to finish reading. Exciting stuff, isn't it?

Wait a minute, isn't this what we used to have in the UK, but admittedly without a view of the beach? Sadly, the last time I visited the UK, my local library had closed and is now a tyre depot. Similarly, many other local libraries are under threat of either closure or have been handed over to well-meaning groups of volunteers who are responsible for maintaining and funding its continued existence.

I have spent most of my working life encouraging children and adults to read, and hopefully nurturing a love of books, as well as teaching how to access relevant information, which has become increasingly important at this time of 'fake news'. No, I don't always mean stuffy old print books, but all manner of electronic media, Kindles, e-readers, iPads and the like.

When a gift is required, my first inclination and preference is always to give a good book, rather than a stuffed toy or a computer game. Does it really matter? Have I really wasted my time (and money)? Does anyone value books and read for pleasure anymore?

What is happening to all those wonderful (and not so wonderful) buildings that used to be a storehouse of magic and information in the UK? Figures from 2017 show that around 500 libraries have closed in England, Scotland and Wales. Whatever happened to the idea of libraries as information points, which include access to computers, as well as books? Not everyone has access to, or can afford a smartphone or a computer.

Knowledgeable and supportive staff are needed to help the elderly, the homeless, and the disadvantaged to access information. One quarter of all library jobs in the UK, which is around 8000 staff, have disappeared over the last few years. I recall the mother of David Cameron, the UK's previous Prime Minister, campaigning vigorously to keep her local library open; so maybe it does matter.

"Ah yes", we are told "this is the result of the recession…" During the same period that libraries closed, around 15,000 volunteers were recruited. As well-meaning as volunteers are, they are no longer appointed to assist full-time, professional staff, but to replace them. As well as exploiting the good nature and willingness of volunteers, it devalues the professionalism and dedication of well-trained, professional and experienced library staff. Presumably, the next step will be to replace full time teachers and nurses with well-meaning volunteers?

When a branch of House of Fraser or Marks and Spencer closes, there is a huge outcry and protests at this "hideous distortion of the High Street", but is there the same outcry and defence of a local library when it is handed over to local volunteers or, worse still, closed? "Oh, we can get it all on line" is the predictable response, but is this true?

A well-run and well-managed library is of tremendous benefit to the whole community. As well as a providing a source of richness and magic, libraries provide easy and ready access to a confusing world of information. I wonder if any reader has applied for the new Universal Credit? I don't know that much about it, but I do know that there are many who cannot access the information simply because they do not have ready access to a smartphone or a computer. A library with trained and knowledgeable staff on hand to provide help and advice is essential in assisting claimants to negotiate the minefield of this benefit.

Libraries also provide solid defence against the modern scourge of loneliness faced by many elderly, as well as younger people. It is a safe space that offers shared experiences and a chance to be with people, as well as keeping warm during those cold winter days, and without having to spend any money.

If libraries didn't already exist, we would be busy inventing them. Thankfully, my experiences in

Spain's libraries tell me that they are mostly valued, well used and comparatively well-funded to their UK counterparts. As for that wonderful Beach Library in Fuerteventura; I cannot wait to visit it.

Timples and Traditions

A Little More than Amnesia

I guess most people have heard of Indonesia and maybe Polynesia, but what about Macaronesia and, indeed, Micronesia? How about visiting Macaronesia one day? No, this is not a new name for France invented by the current ambitious President Macron, but a cluster of four archipelagos in the North Atlantic Ocean, just off the continents of Africa and Europe, which are formed by raised and exposed peaks of the ocean floor that peer out above the ocean's surface.

The Canary Islands are part of Macaronesia, which also includes Cape Verde, Madeira and the Azores. Interestingly, the islands belong to three different countries: Spain, Portugal and Cape Verde, which are all part of the continent of Africa. The Azores are an exception, since they are part of the European continent.

Although I vaguely remember the term 'Macaronesia' being used during geography lessons when I was a pupil, I have rarely heard the term used in recent years. It came to light once again this week after Cape Verde announced that it was aiming for a free trade zone with other Atlantic islands to allow for the free movement of people, as well as goods and services. Despite the term 'free trade area' now being seen as 'dirty words' in the UK during the current UK-EU Brexit negotiations, it is good to hear that the establishment of free trade areas by others is regarded as a very sensible way forward for nations to trade and work together in a coherent and civilised manner.

Cape Verde is a group of ten windswept islands off the coast of West Africa. It is a volcanic archipelago that was a Portuguese colony until 1975, and with which it still has close links. The islands have stronger economic growth that most of the sub-Saharan countries in Africa. The International Monetary Fund recorded Cape Verde's growth in 2017 at 4 per cent, which is forecast to improve even further to around 7 per cent. The islands are hoping to enhance tourism and economic growth with such a deal and re-engaging with other islands in what is known as Macaronesia. Cape Verde is hoping to create a legal framework for its people and goods to travel freely for the benefit of all.

The Cape Verde islands, which have a population of around 500,000, and with a large expat population, have already passed legislation to remove visa requirements for Europeans and hope that the European Union will reciprocate. Laws have been changed to make it easier for foreign investors to invest, and recent legislation allows foreign exchange accounts to fund transfers without restrictions. Cape Verde's currency is linked to the euro, which also facilities business activities. Cape Verde has aspirations to develop the islands as a hub for air travel, since it is ideally located between the Americas, Europe and Africa. It also sees itself as offering great potential as a digital hub for Africa.

Since I mentioned Micronesia at the beginning of this article, I should explain that this group of small islands is in the Pacific Ocean, but that is a story for another time. I think I am going to add Macaronesia to my postal address in future, after several incidents of my post being sent to the Cayman Islands, instead of the Canary Islands. It might help Correos to deliver my post rather more accurately in future.

Celebrating Canaries Day

Fiestas can be a confusing experience for expats living in Spain and the Canary Islands. They tend to creep up on you and there have been many times that I have found shops and offices to be closed when least expected. Municipalities tend to celebrate fiestas on different days, which can also be confusing for workers living in one municipality, but working in another. Fiestas are a way of life in Spain and I often admire the ingenuity with which a fiesta can be linked with a weekend via a 'puente day' (bridging day) to create a very long weekend or even a week off work if the calendar works out correctly!

My favourite fiesta is 'Día de Canarias (Canaries Day), which is celebrated throughout the Canary Islands. The actual day of celebration is 30 May, but celebrated on 29 May, which allows sufficient time to recover from excessive partying during the night before the actual day of celebration. We can happily visit any shop or office in the full knowledge that it will be closed (unless in the tourist areas). At least we all know where we are with this fiesta, and there is little confusion about the date of this big event.

The Canary Islands consist of Gran Canaria, Tenerife, Lanzarote, Fuerteventura, La Gomera, La Palma, El Hierro and the Chinijo Archipelago, which include the islands of La Graciosa, Alegranza, Montaña Clara, Roque del Este and Roque del Oeste. Spain began the conquest of the islands in 1402, which were finally incorporated into the Kingdom of Castile in 1495. On 10 August 1982, the islands were granted autonomous community status within Spain. Canaries

Day is special, since it represents the culmination of long held desires for greater representation and autonomy of the islands within Spain. 30th May 1983 represents the first session of the Canarian Parliament, and was the beginning of a louder voice for the islands.

In the build-up to Canaries Day, Canarian flags are proudly displayed, balconies decorated with flowers and children dressed in their finest traditional Canarian costumes. It is a good time to taste and experience some of the unique Canarian dishes, as well as admiring local crafts. Schools encourage and remind children and local people of Canarian culture and traditions, with many schools holding special classes to remind residents of their place within the islands' history and customs.

In many towns and villages there are special church services, sporting events, food tastings, animal shows, concerts of traditional music, and exhibitions of arts and crafts made by local people. Parties are often held at home or in restaurants on the evening of May 29th, and celebrations continue on the big day itself.

The flying of flags across the islands is also an important part of the celebrations. For British visitors, this can seem unusual, since the British public rarely fly the Union flag, and normally it only appears for formal state and ceremonial occasions, such as Royal weddings. In the Canary Islands, it is common to see the Canarian flag, the Spanish flag and, dare I say, the European Union flag, flying together to represent unity and harmony.

The first flag for the Canary Islands was created in 1961 by a political movement called 'The Free Canary Islands'. The flag is a tricolour of equal vertical bands in white, blue and yellow, with the coat of arms of the Canary Islands on the blue band at the centre of the state flag. Since arguments between the two largest islands, Tenerife and Gran Canaria, have been vociferous in the past, the flag sensibly combines the maritime flags of Tenerife and Gran Canaria, which are the blue and white colours of the Province of Santa Cruz de Tenerife with the blue and yellow colours of the Province of Las Palmas de Gran Canaria.

The placement of the colours is said to correspond with the physical location of the two major islands, with white for Tenerife on the left, representing the island's western location. Yellow, for Gran Canaria, is on the right representing the island's eastern location. The colour blue in the centre of the flag is the common colour for both islands and their provinces.

The coat of arms included on the state flag consists of a blue shield supported by two dogs. The two dogs are a reference to the Latin name 'Insula Canaria', which means 'Island of Dogs', which disappointingly has nothing at all to do with canary birds. There is a red crown at the top of the shield, demonstrating allegiance to Spain's monarchy, and a banner with the word 'Oceano' above the crown. Interestingly, although the islands are not an independent country, the flag can be found as an emoji on some of the more popular smartphone apps, which has created amusement and interest on the islands.

All of Spain's autonomous communities celebrate their special days in ways that are appropriate to their unique culture and traditions. Wherever you are living or staying in Spain, do make an effort to participate and enjoy these special fiestas, since they are intrinsic parts of this amazing, vibrant and colourful country.

Let's Thresh a Lentil

An interesting photographic exhibition in Lanzarote caught my eye this week. The exhibition, which was presented by local students, brought together 300 photographs from the family albums of their grandparents and great grandparents, which reflected life on the island in the last century.

In one photograph, the great grandparents of one student are shown threshing lentils, which were grown on the island. Lentils are usually regarded as one of the world's healthiest foods and it was interesting to see that they were grown and harvested in Lanzarote, as well as the other Canary Islands.

The island of Lanzarote is just sixty miles off the coast of the Sahara. It is a dry and volcanic island, with six to eight inches of rain in a good year and much less during a drought; both this and its volcanic geology became this island's destiny. Serious problems for islanders were caused by volcanic disasters. As with all the Canary Islands, such conditions determined the crops that could be grown to ensure survival in sometimes wretched economic and climatic conditions. One of the answers was to be lentils.

Long before the Spanish conquest of the Canary Islands, people used the rich, fertile earth to grow a range of subsistence crops, which included lentils. The lentil is one of the oldest and hardiest foods in the world, and there is no legume more resistant to arid land than the lentil. It needs very little water to grow and can survive the hottest or coldest of climates.

Lentils originated in central Asia and have been eaten since prehistoric times and are one of the first foods known to be cultivated, since seeds dating back 8000 years have been found in archaeological sites in the Middle East. Archaeologists even discovered traces of lentils buried with the dead in Egyptian pyramids. The humble lentil had reached mythical status and was praised for its ability to enlighten the mind, even in the afterlife. In Catholic countries, such as Spain and the Canary Islands, lentils have long been used as a staple food during Lent.

Lentil stew is a popular dish in the Canary Islands, and often served with potatoes, chorizo and vegetables. I am also told that the addition of garlic croutons and red Canary wine together with crusty bread makes a comforting and wholesome dish, and best found in many of the small, traditional family-run restaurants on the islands. Lentils do not need to be soaked before cooking, have multiple uses in the kitchen, and their flavour enhances any vegetable or meat ingredient. It is no wonder that they have been a treasured foodstuff since early times.

As a vegetarian for many years, I have long been aware of the high nutritional properties of the humble lentil. They are an excellent source of cholesterol-lowering fibre, as well as having an ability to manage blood sugar levels following a meal. Lentils contain seven of the most important minerals, including B-vitamins and protein, and with virtually no fat. Indeed, just a cupful of cooked lentils will set you back around 200 calories, so they are great for anyone on a diet. The fibre content helps to overcome digestive disorders, such as irritable bowel syndrome and prevents constipation. There are also huge benefits to the heart; according to food intake studies, lentils were associated with an 82 per cent reduction in risk from heart attacks due to their fibre, as well as from the significant amounts of folate and magnesium. Lentils are rich in iron and, unlike red meat, are not rich in calories or fat, which makes them ideal for those who require increased levels of iron, including growing children and adolescents.

I am very fond of pasta dishes, but try to avoid eating them too often, because they can be very fattening. I have recently discovered pasta made entirely from lentils, which can now be easily purchased from some of the major supermarkets. At last, I can enjoy pasta without worrying about the calories.

This one old photograph of a couple threshing lentils on this beautiful island reminded me of the immense value of the humble lentil, which can be rightly called "an ancient crop for modern times". If you haven't yet eaten a lentil dish, or used them within a meal, I recommend that you do. As for me, I'm off to enjoy a lentil bake and a glass of red Lanzarote wine for lunch.

Calima - Gone With the Wind

Expats in Spain and the Canary Islands will often hear the words "Oh, it's just a calima" trotted out whenever it is a little cloudy or there is annoying dust in the air. In reality, it is not quite as simple as that, and the true calima is something to be celebrated, as well as to curse, particularly if you suffer from breathing conditions and respiratory allergies.

In the Canary Islands, the calima is often referred to as "Bruma Seca", which is "Dry Fog". It appears for up to ten times each year for a day or two, but in the worst cases, can be present for a week, or even longer. People with respiratory problems and allergies often suffer considerably during these periods. It is a time when sensible people try to stay indoors or wear a face mask when going outside for any length of time if they suffer from breathing conditions.

Calimas are usually, but not always, accompanied by very hot winds, and humidity levels increase. Residents are plagued with reddish dust on their patios and cars, which also invades every crevice of their homes. A calima occurs when dust from the Sahara Desert is dragged across landmass by strong winds. Dust can remain suspended for hours and even days; visibility is reduced and the air becomes cloudy as a result of the dust.

The Canary Islands are often regarded as having the "best climate in the world", but we are not immune from the devastating effects of calimas. The intensity of heat on the islands increases respiratory problems and allergies, as well as general oral health. The tiny particles of dust generated irritates the mucous membranes, which can have serious implications for oral health. Often, as a result of taking antihistamines to control allergies, the immune system fills the hollows of our head with mucus. The cavities that are located above the mouth cause pain and greater sensitivity to cold and heat when filled with mucus, because of increased pressure upon the upper teeth.

Calimas are not all bad, since the Central Sahara was a lake in prehistoric times. The dry sand contains fertile remains of its once rich, organic particles. These nitrogen-rich components within a calima help to fertilise the Atlantic Ocean by promoting the growth of phytoplankton, which forms the basis of the food chain that allows all sea creatures to survive and thrive. Climate change scientists believe that the greenhouse effect is minimised, because the sea's micro-organisms absorb harmful carbon dioxide from the atmosphere. In other words, the more phytoplankton in the sea, the less carbon dioxide in the air. However, it is a delicate balance and too much dust in the Atlantic could create too much plankton and areas of low oxygen, which is not so good.

According to researchers, calima dust from the Sahara also helps to feed plants in the Amazon, since it acts as a fertiliser, which helps the rain forest to grow and thrive. There are also other complex interactions linking calimas to events that we do not yet fully understand. Some studies claim that the damage of hurricanes is reduced due to the effect of calimas cooling the water temperature that is needed for hurricanes to build. Around one third of the natural soils that make up the Canary Islands are based upon

Saharan dust that has dropped on the islands over millennia. The rich, fertile soils on these islands have been enriched through the effects of the calima.

Many suffer from the health effects of the calima, or complain about the dust that has landed on their patios and cars. Maybe we should instead be grateful that it is feeding the luscious plants in the Amazon rain forest, fertilising the Atlantic Ocean for sea creatures to survive, as well as reducing the greenhouse effect that has such serious implications for us all.

Documentoscopia

I really have no time for graffiti of any kind. I don't care whether it has been daubed by that anonymous street artist or vandal, depending upon your view of life, going under the name of Banksy, or if it is Juan or Maria who feel the urge to scrawl their names in appalling handwriting on a newly painted wall. Admittedly, some graffiti can be extremely artistic, amusing, challenging, controversial, but please let us have it on spaces allocated for just that purpose.

Although graffiti is illegal and considered as vandalism in law, some people consider it to be art, because it is a way that people can express themselves and let their voices be heard. Graffiti can be used as artistic expression, or a form of communication and may be best described as drawings or paintings that have been scribbled, scratched or painted, usually illegally, on a wall or other surface, often within public view and is one of the most common and spatial forms of artistic expression.

For many, it is the very act of illegality that is the main attraction. Graffiti writers take over blank (and preferably newly painted) surfaces, which they use as the canvas for new images. Those who study such things consider it to be a 'sub culture' and a means of expressing individuality, social and political concerns, as well as some of the most innermost feelings.

In Spain and the Canary Islands, spaces surrounding unsightly areas that are ready for eventual development are often given to specific and proven 'street artists' or students as a showcase to demonstrate their artistic skills.

These efforts are often inspiring and a pleasure to look at, but the 'Maria loves Juan' statement scrawled across a badly formed heart on a newly painted wall of a nearby shopping centre is little more than vandalism.

Frankly, if that is the best that Juan can come up with to demonstrate his undying affection for his girl, Maria would be well advised to call off the entanglement right away, and look for someone with a few more brain cells and rather more promising artistic ability.

It pleased many locals recently when police in Arrecife, Lanzarote, decided to act against the widespread graffiti across their city. This new action by police has enabled them to identify 15 local people who have been responsible for causing around 300 acts of graffiti vandalism on public and private property, such as on doors, windows, walls, public benches, canopies and pavements.

As well as annoying, some claim that they have caused some degradation of the island's rich heritage.

Interestingly, and all would-be graffiti vandals may wish to note this, the island's police have invested in a special unit known as 'Documentoscopia', or writing style analysis. This unit was brought into use following many complaints from local residents.

Police use an advanced technology called graphonomics that identifies these 'graffiti artists' by determining the artistic styles. Police can now successfully identify and prosecute the author of graffiti, which has previously gone unchecked.

At the present time, penalties for acts of vandalism are around 600 euros, so would-be Banksys who do not have deep pockets would be well advised to practice somewhere other than Lanzarote.

Anyone for a Timple?

"How about a timple?" I was asked by an earnest assistant in one of the traditional music shops in Las Palmas. I had just called in for a replacement violin string, and was looking at the range of Canarian traditional stringed instruments for sale. I quickly realised that I was not being offered an early morning alcoholic drink, and that the young salesman, speaking in English, had discovered an amusing way to catch the attention of English-speaking visitors to the shop.

I have only recently begun to study early Canarian musical instruments, and as my first passion is the violin, this particular stringed instrument caught my eye, simply because of the beauty and simplicity of design.

The timple creates a voice by the instrumentalist plucking its strings in much the same way as the guitar, but there the similarity ends. It is much smaller than the guitar and usually has five strings, although in Tenerife some timples only have four strings.

The timple is mainly used to accompany Canarian folk music and has a loud and rather sharp voice. Due to the success and increasing popularity of this instrument, it has now reached the status of a solo instrument in some circles.

The name of the instrument still intrigues me and I have yet to find a definitive answer to the origin of its name.

In line with my initial thought about an alcoholic drink, the timple did used to be called a tiple (with only one 'p'); before that it was called a 'camelito camelillo' because the back of the instrument looks very much like the hump of a camel, although it is less than 40 centimetres in length.

Timples were created in the Nineteenth Century and played throughout the Canary Islands and much of South America. In many ways, they are related to the ukulele, the Spanish guitar and the Portuguese chavaquino.

Interestingly, the range of woods used is varied with the most common being pine for the body, ebony for the bridges, holy stick for the mast, and wood from the orange tree for decoration.

Creation of these beautiful and interesting instruments was and still is a cottage industry across the islands, offering considerable variation in both design and construction.

The island of Lanzarote became the centre for the systematic making of these instruments where one of the last timple makers is about to retire after more than sixty years of timple making.

The Government of Lanzarote has recognised Antonio Lemes Herandez as artisan of the year for his involvement for more than half a century in the production of timples.

Antonio, a craftsman from Teguise, has been building small timples since he was a child. As a child, he made them from cardboard and other materials before painting them. He eventually perfected his technique and transformed a range of wood into his instruments, mostly pine, which he favours for timples since it can tune well.

Over the years, Antonio has developed his own unique house style, which continues to delight players across the islands and across the world. Sixty years after his first contact with the timple, Antonio's hands continue to create his unique timples, although he now feels that it is time to retire.

There are many renowned timplistas, as timple players are referred to, playing classical music and jazz and it is often regarded as an alternative instrument of choice chosen by guitarists. During the next fiesta, if you are fortunate enough to hear Canarian instrumentalists, do watch out for and listen carefully to the timple. I am sure that, like me, you will find it to be an engaging and fascinating instrument.

Lizards, Lottery and Lanzarote

Getting to Know a Lizard

She rested silently on the dry, stone wall watching me with her black eyes, studying my every move with careful precision. Her slender body soaking up every ray of the brilliant, warming sun. The long tongue flicked out of her mouth as she savoured every tasty morsel that came her way.

For a lizard, Clemmy is of diminutive size, and I am convinced that she has hardly grown over the three years that I have known her. She only appears on hot, sunny days, when the sun's rays hit the same spot on the wall of our garden. She usually appears when I am pruning the roses, setting new plants or watering the garden. I talk to her and she appears to listen carefully to my every word; goodness knows what the neighbours think of our conversations. Sometimes, I give Clemmy a small piece of fruit, which she enjoys, and there is always a little water dripping from a tap that needs a new washer, so I know that she does not lack liquid refreshment.

I am not an expert on lizards, so I am unsure as to what species Clemmy is, but these islands are home to some of the most impressive lizards on the planet. It is interesting to know that most of the Canary Islands have their own indigenous species and may best be regarded as a lizard paradise. The islands of Gran Canaria, Tenerife, La Gomera, La Palma and El Hierro are home to some of the largest true lizards on the planet that can grow to around 80 centimetres long, so Clemmy has a very long way to go.

The Giant Gran Canaria Lizard (Gallotia stehleni) is a common sight all over the island if we are quiet and take care to look for them. Lizards are curious, nosey creatures that many visitors and locals simply do not see. Their disguise is superb and they can easily blend into their rocky surroundings.

Fortunately, they are a protected species by law and it is illegal to catch or kill lizards. Sadly, giant lizards are either extinct or severely endangered on the other Canary Islands, since they have been heavily hunted over the years by cats and rats and other predators. Sadly, the release of captive snakes in recent years by thoughtless pet owners has led to a reduction in the lizard population, since snakes find lizards to be a tasty addition to their diet.

The Giant Gran Canaria lizard is not to be argued with, since they have a very determined bite if provoked. Although they never attack humans, they do chase and fight their own kind. It is also true that lizards grow new tails if their original one gets damaged or bitten off by a predator.

I am reminded that 14 August is World Lizard Day, and that I have the privilege to share an island with thousands of lizards that have made the islands their home long before man became the imposter in their lives. Lizards, like Clemmy, are the true Canarians and deserve to be free and to roam as they please.

Win a House for Five Euros!

I have never liked gambling or entered a betting office, and I do not buy lottery tickets. Indeed, the only gambling that I confess to was spending a quarter in a slot machine in Las Vegas many years ago, since my fascination with the technology on display in that fascinating 'hell on earth' was a temptation that I could not avoid.

My reasons are simple and based upon the Quaker principles that I have always admired and tried to follow, with varying degrees of success I might add. I have always believed that gambling is similar to currency speculation and dealing in stocks and shares; some people gain at the expense of others who often cannot afford to take a loss. I refuse to bet on dogs and horses too, simply because of the cruelty that is always involved when animals are used and exploited for sport. Few horse racing enthusiasts realise that the beautiful horse that they fondly placed a bet on will end up in a tin of dog food when its racing and stud days are over.

My own dealings with an animal charity in the UK that has a focus on rescuing greyhounds that were of no more use on the racetrack, and were simply disposed of, was just one experience that confirmed my belief. No doubt some will dismiss my views as both simplistic and unrealistic, but we all have moral choices and decisions to make in life. Despite my objection to gambling, I was fascinated to read that I had an opportunity to buy a home in Spain for just 5 euros when a flyer dropped through our letterbox last week.

"This is the opportunity to have your dream home in the sun - for only 5 euros" screamed the headline. This was a raffle offering an opportunity to win a fully refurbished home, with 200 square metres of space, two bedrooms, bathroom, storage room, basement, living room, dining room, kitchen and sun terrace. This lovely residence is set in a pretty village, just minutes from the beach and the mountains. How could I, or anyone, refuse such an offer? Upon further investigation, I discovered that there are 70,000 raffle tickets and if all are sold, the owner will earn 350,000 euros, less expenses, which is not a bad return on a property that I suspect is worth considerably less.

The idea is simple, and is a pioneering business in Spain that is dedicated to raffling off unwanted properties. After the recession, there were and still are many unwanted properties in Spain. Some are mortgage foreclosures that have been reclaimed by the banks, whilst others are properties belonging to those whose circumstances in life have changed, such as redundancy, illness, death of a partner or relationship breakdown. Many people feel trapped in their homes, because they have been unable to sell their properties. Traditional buyers of properties often find it difficult to raise the 20 per cent deposit that banks require for a mortgage, and the lottery idea seems to have created new hope for many would-be sellers, as well as potential buyers.

Raffling off properties seems to be a growing trend in parts of the country with buyers participating from all over the world. The lottery company charges for a personalised website, consultancy, raffle publicity and the legalities of the operation. The winner of the lottery takes the house, and all costs associated with changing the name on the deeds are covered by the owner.

It does seem to be an interesting and creative idea, which has gained the approval of the Spanish Housing and Finance Ministries. Maybe it is not a good idea to invest your life savings in buying tickets, but I guess that the odd five euros can do no harm. If any reader has used a lottery to sell their property, or maybe won their home in this way, do please let me know.

The Motor of the Atlantic Ocean

I like visiting churches, and particularly the old ones. Not only are they an ideal place to rest for a few minutes, but they charge my spiritual batteries, allow me to cool down from the heat of the sun and teach me quite a lot about the people that live and worship within the local community.

Until recently, I have rarely considered the physical positioning of church buildings, and always assumed that much was subject to the availability of suitable land, as well as the positioning of other buildings and natural features. In other words, I have assumed that most churches were built more by accident rather than focussed design.

A recent study in the Canary Islands has made me realise that there is much more to the subject and, once again, reminded me that the trade winds had, and continue to have, an important part to play in the history and development of these islands.

The trade winds have both a positive and negative impact upon everything in the Canary Islands. The shape of the volcanoes, climate, the guiding of sailing boats and the natural cycles that enrich the Atlantic Ocean are all affected by the trade winds, which many refer to as "the Motor of the Atlantic Ocean".

Mariners have used and relied upon them for centuries for reliable and swift sailing. Surprisingly, the trade winds may also have determined how churches were originally built in the Canary Islands.

Three researchers from the Institute of Astronomy and Space Physics of Buenos Aires, the Institute of Astrophysics of the Canary Islands and the Institute of Heritage Sciences of Santiago de Compostela have carried out a very interesting study of 32 churches across the Canary Islands and have recently reported their findings.

Most Christian churches in Europe were for centuries built with an orientation that would allow the priest to look to the east when officiating at the Mass. This instruction came from the first Council of Nicea in 325 AD.

In most churches, the altar is aligned to the point where the sun rises, which followed the advice given by Saint Athanasius of Alexandria in the Fourth Century, which was designed to allow worshippers to hear the Mass whilst facing the sun.

Later, Church law stated that church buildings must observe the principles and norms of the Bible and sacred art, so that many churches have their nave facing east or towards the point where the sun rose on the day of the year when its foundations were laid.

This practice was followed in almost all Christian churches in the world, with the exception of those in North Africa, where churches tend to face west.

Current researchers wanted to discover if this North African custom could be seen in the first Christian churches of the Canary Islands, because of the influence of the aborigines of the islands, who descended from the Berber villages of North Africa.

They examined the orientation of churches in Lanzarote, the island where the European presence is older and goes back almost a century before the conquest of Gran Canaria or Tenerife was completed.

The research findings were surprising, since the orientation of the oldest churches of Lanzarote does not show a clear influence of the aboriginal culture that can be attributed to ancient cults of these people, or their knowledge of astronomy.

This was particularly interesting, because several pre-Hispanic sites across the Canary Islands mark the sunrise in the solstices and equinoxes, which allowed aboriginal societies to have a calendar for rituals, sowing and harvesting.

Of the thirty-two churches analysed, all were built between the Sixteenth and Nineteenth Centuries.

Seventeen are positioned to face east at sunrise, one is almost exactly aligned with the equinoxes (Nuestra Señora de las Mercedes in Mala) and two more were built in reverse, looking west. However, twelve were aligned to face in a north-north easterly direction.

These researchers conclude that this peculiarity of Lanzarote churches is unique in all of Europe. They suggest that it is a compromise response to a cultural combination of beliefs of the aborigines and the faith of their conquerors.

Some churches in the Canary Islands show a marked difference to the orientation of nearly all Christian churches across the world and could have been influenced by the direction of trade winds that were so important to the aboriginal people living in these islands. So, next time that you visit a church in the Canary Islands, do take a compass with you.

Lottery and Lanzarote

In the United States, a South Carolina ticket holder recently claimed the biggest lottery win in the history of the country, and with the lottery company confirming that there is one winner of the US$1.6 billion prize, which is about 1.2 billion pounds, all for just a two-dollar stake. Admittedly, the odds of winning were not great at one in more than 300 million, but maybe it was worth taking the risk of loss in this particular case.

In Spain and the Canary Islands, we are approaching that time of the year when tickets for the annual Christmas Lottery are on sale. This particular lottery, which is more commonly known as 'El Gordo' (The Big/Fat One) is very important in Spain, and towns and villages grind to a halt during the morning of the 22nd December when children 'sing' the lottery numbers in the usual tuneless monotone, which is traditional of the event. The roll call of numbers seems to go on for hours, and the doleful dirge stays with listeners for much of the day. It is one of those sounds, rather like an annoying advertising jingle, that is hard to forget. In Spain, the Christmas Lottery is an essential part of Christmas and is, for many, when Christmas celebrations truly begin.

There was also another special lottery this year, which was to celebrate Spain's National Day on 12 October ('Especial Día de la Hispanidad de la Lotorería Nacional). This lottery, offered 84 million euros in prizes, which meant even more to Canary Islanders this year, and particularly those living in, as well as those who have a particular connection to, the island of Lanzarote. The Plaza de Los Leones de Teguise in Lanzarote was the scene for this year's prize draw. This special issue consisted of 100,000 tickets, divided into tickets of 120 euros. Each ticket was sub divided into tickets costing 12 euros each.

Teguise was the previous capital of Lanzarote for 450 years until 1852, when it was supplanted by the 'modern upstart' Arrecife. Teguise remains an important cultural and tourist centre with its streets brimming with convents, squares and palaces. The town was named after the last Princess of the native, pre-Spanish inhabitants, called Guanches, and is the oldest Spanish settlement in the entire Canary Islands, dating back to 1402. This beautiful town witnessed many attacks by pirates, as well as the Moors and Christians, which reached its climax in 1618, with an invasion of 5000 Algerian buccaneers who overran the town, which led to a violent massacre.

In the 1980s, great efforts were made to restore Teguise to its former glory and to recognise its status as one of the oldest towns in the Canary Islands. As such, the town was declared to be an important architectural and historic site, since it is where much of Lanzarote's vibrant history has been written.

Today, many locals and tourists visit the town, particularly during the morning hours, but the best time to see this architectural treasure is when they have gone home for lunch. Once the hustle and bustle of bargain hunters have disappeared, deserted streets create a unique flavour of Teguise's prosperous, yet more troublesome past. Thankfully, few organised coach tours show much interest in the town, and the lack of hotels helps to ensure that Teguise remains frozen in time.

The decision to highlight Lanzarote in this way was an enlightened one designed to mark and celebrate the 600th anniversary of a very special town. Hopefully, there were many happy lottery prize winners in Lanzarote this year; if not, there is always another lottery just around the corner.

Printed in Poland
by Amazon Fulfillment
Poland Sp. z o.o., Wrocław